Why Some Companies Emerge Stronger and Better from a Crisis

Why Some Companies Emerge Stronger and Better from a Crisis

7 Essential Lessons for Surviving Disaster

Ian I. Mitroff

American Management Association

New York • Atlanta • Brussels • Chicago • Mexico City • San Francisco
Shanghai • Tokyo • Toronto • Washington, D.C.

*Special discounts on bulk quantities of AMACOM books are available to corporations, professional associations, and other organizations. For details, contact Special Sales Department, AMACOM, a division of American Management Association, 1601 Broadway, New York, NY 10019.
Tel.: 212-903-8316. Fax: 212-903-8083.
Web site: www.amacombooks.org*

Library of Congress Cataloging-in-Publication Data

Mitroff, Ian I.
Why some companies emerge stronger and better from a crisis : 7 essential lessons for surviving disaster / Ian I. Mitroff.
p. cm.
Includes index.
ISBN 0-8144-0850-8 (hardcover)
1. Crisis management. 2. Emergency management. 3. Leadership. I. Title.

HD49.M572 2005
658.4'056—dc22 *2004019226*

Printing number
10 9 8 7 6 5 4 3 2 1

This book is dedicated to Chris and to Vince, who have helped me to get stronger and better.

Contents

*Un*certainty [italics in original] is the only certainty now—in politics and terror.

Jonathan Alter, *Newsweek*, April 19, 2004, p. 42

Preface

America's organizations and institutions are in dire trouble on every conceivable front: physically, intellectually, morally, and spiritually. First, their operations, plants, and infrastructure have been the objects of direct terrorist attacks and other serious criminal threats. Second, the (intellectual) foundations—that is, the fundamental assumptions upon which their crisis plans and procedures are based—have been seriously undermined, if not proven false, by recent events. Third, their moral compasses have been eroded by an unprecedented series of corporate scandals, such as Enron/Andersen, Martha Stewart, Tyco, and the like. And, fourth, they have not only been oblivious of, but actually destructive with regard to, the spiritual needs of their employees and customers. In short, America's organizations and institutions are in crisis, big time. In fact, they are under attack as never before.

The surveys that my colleague Dr. Murat Alpaslan and I have conducted have shown that prior to 9/11, corporate America was basically unprepared for a wide variety of crises, especially with regard to terrorism. Even worse, corporate America is still largely unprepared, some four years after 9/11. This situation stands in sharp contrast to people who have lived through a major crisis. Invariably, they will say that they wished they had had *more, not less*, preparation for meeting the extreme challenges that crises present.

By definition, a crisis for an organization is an extreme event that literally threatens its very existence. At the very least, it causes substantial injuries, deaths, and financial costs, as well as serious damage to its corporate reputation. Yet those individuals, organizations, and societies that have successfully weathered major crises have learned the major lessons that crises have to teach, and they have emerged even stronger and better than they were before.

Unfortunately, most executives and most organizations are prepared at best for a limited number of crises, mainly fires and natural disasters. A few organizations may even be prepared for direct threats to their core business, such as food contamination or product tampering, but even this situation is not as widespread as it should be. Furthermore, those businesses that do prepare for crises such as food contamination or product tampering are doing so mainly in their primary industries, as in the food and pharmaceutical industries.

Why Some Companies Emerge Stronger and Better from a Crisis presents seven essential challenges that all organizations, public and private, for profit and not for profit, need to face and overcome if they are to survive today's threats. In meeting and overcoming these challenges, successful crisis leaders have learned, even if they have not completely mastered, seven essential lessons. Learning these lessons can help everyone to anticipate, plan for, and survive the crises that are an inevitable part of life.

Seven Essential Lessons for Overcoming the Challenges of Crisis Management

Crises challenge us to develop and to practice the following:

1. *Right heart.* Crises exact tremendous emotional costs; as a result, crises demand exceptional emotional capabilities, or emotional IQ. Effective crisis management (CM) demands high emotional capacity (e.g., sensitivity) and emotional resiliency; without these, the vast majority of people are emotionally incapacitated by major crises, some for life.

2. *Right thinking.* Crises demand that we be capable of exercising on-the-spot creative thinking. They demand that we are capable of thinking "*outside of the box that contains the box!*"; this is known as *double outside of the box thinking*—in short, effective CM demands high creative IQ;

3. *Right soul.* Effective CM requires a special type of inner spiritual growth, or spiritual IQ. Without this, our world is rendered meaningless by a major crisis. Many lose the will to live and regain purpose to their lives; in short, most major crises cause a person to suffer an additional crisis, a deep existential crisis. Nothing devastates the soul as much as a crisis.

4. *Right social and political skills.* Effective CM requires a special type of political and social IQ. This is absolutely necessary if we are to get the leaders of an organization to buy into CM.

5. *Right technical skills.* Crises demand that we know different things and that we do things differently; this is technical IQ. For instance, to outwit terrorists, we have to learn to think like a controlled paranoid without becoming either a full-fledged terrorist, a paranoid, or a psychopath.

6. ***Right integration.*** **Effective CM requires that we integrate previous forms of IQ; thus, integrative IQ is required. The recognition of this and how to accomplish an integrative IQ is one of the most important and distinguishing marks of this book.**

7. ***Right transfer.*** **This book is about a lot more than just CM; it is also about the new skills that are needed in the global economy. Without integrative IQ, more and more white-collar and professional jobs will be lost; without integrative IQ, the United States will become a jobless economy. New knowledge and new forms of IQ are needed; I call this aesthetic IQ, for it allows us to see the world anew.**

Crisis leadership is not just good for business—that is, the proverbial bottom line—it is also necessary for the existential, emotional, and spiritual bottom line. No person, no business, no organization, no institution, no society can survive for long without crisis leadership.

About This Book

Starting with Chapter Two, this book presents a single major challenge met by individuals and companies that have successfully managed and survived major crises. The only exception to this rule is Chapter Three, which presents two challenges since they are closely related. In addition, Chapter Nine explains how all of these lessons apply to something as complex as society as a whole. Mastering the challenges allows everyone to become a crisis leader in his or her organization.

The book is based on scores of interviews conducted prior to 9/11, immediately after, and three years subsequent to it. In addition, it is based on an ongoing series of interviews with politicians, government officials, corporate executives, senior managers, ordinary citizens, and members of public interest groups. It is also based on my work of over twenty-five years in the field of CM, of which I am one of the founders.

All of the cases described in this book are based on actual situations. However, except where noted, the names of the people and organizations have been changed or combined into composites. Especially in today's world, companies are extremely afraid and reluctant to identify what they are doing in order to protect themselves. Their fears of becoming prime targets are legitimate.

Why Some Companies Emerge Stronger and Better from a Crisis is not primarily a nuts and bolts book. Although it delves into the details of CM, it is much more concerned with the proper attitudes—the underlying philosophy—that we need to cultivate if CM is to be successful. Indeed, if these attitudes are missing, then the nuts and bolts will not work. An overemphasis on nuts and bolts and neglect of the proper attitudes and philosophy with which CM must be practiced actually help cause or exacerbate major crises. Thus, this book delves beneath the surface of everyday behavior. It examines and critiques the assumptions upon which our behavior stands, but that are rarely challenged. Yet it is assumptions, and not tools or techniques, that are the heart of CM. This emphasis on assumptions is what makes this book different from virtually all other books on CM, including those by this author.

I have adopted this approach because CM is in danger of a "hostile takeover" by risk management (RM) and business continuity planning (BCP). Indeed, RM and BCP threaten to reduce CM to a series of structured exercises and checklists. The compulsive need for structure and certainty has led far too many organizations to buy into the techniques of RM and BCP. This is not to say that RM and BCP are useless. Rather, without an understanding of what CM entails (see Appendix B), RM and BCP can actually do more harm than good. In a word, RM and BCP are not comprehensive and systemic enough, which is precisely what CM needs to be.

I also need to stress that no single individual or organization practices every lesson presented in this book for overcoming the challenges of crises. Instead, I have assembled the best lessons drawn from a wide variety of companies and organizations. This book thus represents a benchmark, a standard, to which all organizations need to aspire.

Finally, this book uses a lot of diagrams and charts. I caution the reader not to be put off by them. In every case, I have made them as simple as I could. I am a visual person. In part, this is because I was trained as a structural engineer, and if structural engineers do anything, they make lots of sketches to explain difficult concepts.

Acknowledgments

The people who have helped me in the conception and writing of this book are far too many for me to list. I would, however, especially like to thank my wife Donna for all her encouragement and critical comments. For over forty years, she has been not only a wonderful spouse but also my best friend. In a world full of crises and betrayals, my wife and immediate family are constant beacons of hope and love.

Finally, I would like to thank my administrative assistant, Terry Scott. Terry did much more than merely type the manuscript; she corrected my many errors in thinking and in organization as well. I also want to acknowledge Terry's invaluable assistance in preparing Appendix A.

Why Some Companies Emerge Stronger and Better from a Crisis

CHAPTER ONE

The Crisis Society: The Rise of the Abnormal

The dogmas of the quiet past are inadequate to the stormy present. The occasion is piled high with difficulty, and we must rise to the occasion. As our case is new, so we must think anew.

—Abraham Lincoln, signing the July 2, 1862, Morrill Act of Congress providing for the state land grant colleges

The Argument

1. Over the last 24 months, there has been a precipitous growth in the sheer number of major crises. Even more ominous, the number of crises has exceeded that of any previous period in the last twenty years.
2. The number of crises not only is growing rapidly but, of even greater concern, is the fact that *the rate* of increase in the number of crises is *increasing* as well. Furthermore, the time, and even the geographical distance, between crises is shrinking precipitously.
3. In addition to the growth in the number of major crises, the extent and pervasiveness of these crises are especially troubling. No major industry, no institution, no segment of society has been spared. Every industry, virtually every institution, and every level of society has experienced major crises. We have become a crisis-plagued society. Our deepest fear is that we have become a crisis-prone society—that is, that the potential for experiencing large-scale major crises has become a permanent and irreversible feature of modern societies.
4. Something even more ominous is afoot. The nature of crises—that is, the types of crises and their qualities—has changed dramatically. Crises have gone from "normal systems accidents"—that is, unintentional system break*downs* due to the overwhelming complexity of modern technologies (e.g., Chernobyl)—to the deliberate, intentional break*up* of organizations, institutions, and even society itself (e.g., 9/11). We have gone from

normal systems accidents to abnormal systems disasters—that is, to planned catastrophes.

5. Normal systems accidents have also changed dramatically. Twenty years ago, normal accidents were mainly confined to single industries. Normal accidents mainly occurred *within* a single company or industry. Now, because of the extreme coupling and interdependency of modern societies, normal accidents now occur *between* different industries and segments of society.
6. Traditional management is poorly equipped to handle intentionally planned catastrophes. It can barely handle normal systems accidents. Indeed, traditional management is a big part of the problem—it is not the solution. As a result, a radically different approach to crisis management (CM) is desperately needed.
7. The abnormal has become the new normal state of affairs.

Long before she got to her office door, Mary Douglas, CEO of Rural Books, could hear that her phone was ringing nonstop. It had a nasty and ominous sound. As soon as she opened her office door, Mary saw that her answering machine was lit up like a Christmas tree. It was filled to capacity. She had already had sixteen calls, and it wasn't even 6:30 A.M.

It was not a good omen. It was, in fact, the beginning of a long nightmare.

A Major Crisis at Rural Books

Headquartered in Montana, Mary had established Rural Books about ten years ago. RB, as its loyal fans called it, produced a highly successful line of field books and guides for identifying and cooking wild fruit, nuts, berries, and the like. Both the books and the guides were extremely popular with rural and city folks alike.

On any weekend, thousands of people could be seen walking in the woods with their trusted RBs at their sides. The books and guides were not only lightweight but also extremely easy to carry and to use. For instance, carrying straps were attached to the bindings of the books so that they could easily be slung over a person's shoulder. They were also designed and manufactured to hold up to extreme elements. Most of all, they were organized around user-friendly pullouts. They not only showed which things were edible and tasty but where they could be found as well.

RB's books were especially known for their clear and simple pictures of the wild foods that were safe to eat versus those that were unsafe. The safe foods were clearly labeled and located on one page while those that were unsafe were located on a completely separate page. The pages even had different colors: green for safe and red for dangerous or unsafe. In this way, RB helped to ensure that there would be no confusion whatsoever. In the ten years of RB's existence, no one had ever suffered any illness from following their recommendations.

Mary picked up the phone. Robert Turnbull, Senior Executive VP and the head of RB's East Coast division, was on the line. He was half shouting and mumbling at the same time. There were unmistakable signs of stress and panic in his voice. Though he was typically calm and easygoing, this was a significant departure from his usual behavior. Mary had in fact never heard him sound more distressed in the five years that they had worked together.

"Mary, have you seen CNN this morning? They are running a story linking us to the deaths of a family of four. The parents were in their early thirties; the kids were just two and three. CNN is also reporting that we are responsible for the serious illness of scores of others. At this time, no one knows the full extent of the injuries. It could be in the hundreds.

"CNN is saying that people became seriously ill after eating poisonous berries. They are claiming that we mislabeled some of the pages in our books. They are also saying something that makes no sense at all. They are saying that it's a case of product tampering. Hell, we don't make food or pharmaceutical products. What is there to tamper with?

"That's all I can tell you at this time. I don't know anything more myself. I have our production and security people checking into it, but what do we say and do in the meantime? I'm getting calls from CNN, the *Wall Street Journal*, the *New York Times*, our investment brokers, everyone. It's complete pandemonium here. They are asking tough questions that I don't have the answers to like, 'Was it a terrorist group, a group of disgruntled employees? Can you in fact rule out any of these possibilities at this time? Was it an intentional act of sabotage? Are the reports of labor troubles at RB true?' What do we say and do? I need help fast!"

Mary's mind was reeling. All she could do was mumble, "I'll get back." RB was prepared for fires and explosions that could burn down its offices and ruin its production facilities, but not for anything like this. The possibility of product tampering, let alone terrorism and disgruntled employees, had never crossed Mary's mind. And yet, she recalled that radical environmental groups had recently been making claims that RB was endangering the environment because of all the people who were trampling—or as they put it, "loving to death"—pristine areas. A few had even sent threatening letters to RB, but she had quickly dismissed them as cranks. She recollected that local militia groups were making threats as well because too many people were wandering too close to their compounds.

"Oh my God," Mary exclaimed, "What am I going to do? I don't have the foggiest clue as to where to begin."

Why RB Was Unable to Meet the Challenges of a Major Crisis

Because Mary and her top team had never received the proper training in crisis management (CM), they were unable to think outside the box. As a result, they were unable to imagine and anticipate the particular types of product tampering that were directly applicable to their business. For instance, were the labels of the foods that were safe to eat versus those that were unsafe intentionally or accidentally reversed when the pages were typeset? Either case—that is, intentionally or accidentally reversing the labels of the pages—is a *form* of product tampering that applies directly to the book business. Altering key information in a product when this information is crucial to the safety and the well-being of people *is* a major form of product tampering. In other words, product tampering is *not* confined to the alteration of food or pharmaceuticals.

In addition, if Mary and her top team had received proper training, they would have been especially prepared for the strong and often overwhelming emotions that are a critical part of every major crisis. Events like 9/11, Enron/Andersen, the Catholic Church, Martha Stewart, NASA, and a seemingly endless series of crises in recent years demonstrate clearly that crises exact a severe emotional toll on those who experience or are part of them.

The costs of crises are severe not only in terms of dollars but also in terms of emotional distress. Those who have been through major crises often use the exact same words to describe their experiences as do soldiers who have been in battle and have suffered severe trauma.

If Mary and her team had faced the challenges, and hence, learned the lessons that successful crisis leaders have to teach, then they would have been able to respond faster and better and thereby have lowered substantially both the economic and the emotional costs of the crisis or crises that they were facing. This does *not* mean that RB would never experience a major crisis at all. In today's world there are no such guarantees. On the contrary, *every* organization is virtually guaranteed to experience at least one major crisis in its history. It merely means that Mary and her top team would have recovered sooner and with far fewer costs.

We're going to use the example of RB throughout this book to illustrate what Mary, her top executives, and, indeed, her entire company could have done differently both to have anticipated and to have prepared for major crises of any kind. (There is no shortage of other examples from the food industry that could have been used. For instance, all of the copies of the April 2004 issue of *Southern Living* magazine had to be pulled from the shelves because of a defective recipe. When mixed as directed, the cooking ingredients set off a highly explosive fire.)

The first thing that Mary and her company should have done is understand what is fundamentally different about today's world, that crises are literally built into the fabric of modern societies.

The Failure of Conventional Ways of Thinking

America's organizations and institutions have become veritable breeding grounds for crises of all kinds. It's obvious, looking at (just to name a few) Ford/Firestone, Enron/Andersen, the Catholic Church, American Airlines, WorldCom, Martha Stewart, the explosion of the Space Shuttle *Columbia* (NASA), or mad cow disease, that conventional management is of little use in either coping with or preventing major crises. Indeed, conventional methods are largely responsible for causing major crises. (In brief, conventional methods are too "rational" to anticipate and to cope with "abnormal states of mind.") And if this weren't bad enough, then 9/11 shows that whole societies are now vulnerable to new forms of major crises as well—that is, state-sponsored terrorism.

Until quite recently, businesses thought of accidents as either "natural" or "normal." Natural disasters—like fires and floods—have been around forever, and most companies know how to use risk-management techniques to protect themselves against them. In contrast, in his important and influential 1984 book *Normal Accidents: Living with High-Risk Technologies*, the distinguished sociologist Charles Perrow defined normal accidents as unintentional failures of systems because of their inherent complexity.[1] Modern technologies have become so complex that the potential for large-scale industrial catastrophes is literally built into their basic design and everyday operations. Industrial disasters like Three Mile Island, Chernobyl, Bhopal, and *Exxon Valdez* were not random aberrations but normal system-overload and malfunction problems.

Preparing for normal accidents is challenging, to put it mildly. Nonetheless, over time many companies have developed coping strategies, such as regularly getting together designers, operators, and maintenance managers of complex systems to compare notes. If the operators are experiencing conditions that aren't in line with the designers' assumptions, then a normal accident is in the offing.

But in the last few years, a new and more ominous category

of crises has emerged. I term these "abnormal accidents." These are intentional accidents that are the result of deliberate acts of evil. They include bombings, kidnappings, cyberattacks, cheating, stealing, manipulation of the truth, and so on. These are accidents caused by betrayal and sabotage, whether by employees or outsiders. Especially since 9/11, it is apparent that preparing for these sorts of events is no longer something that can be put off.

The key difference between normal and abnormal accidents is as follows: normal accidents represent the *unintentional breakdown* of complex technical and organizational systems. In contrast, abnormal accidents represent the *intentional* break*up* of complex technical, organizational, and social systems. (See Table 1-1 for a more complete listing of the differences between normal and abnormal accidents.)

While hardly unheard of in the past, the number of abnormal accidents has risen sharply in the past ten years. Indeed, my analyses[2] suggest that there were at least as many abnormal crises in the past ten years as there were normal. (See Figure 1-1; Appendix A provides a summary of these events.) In addition, the impact of Enron/Andersen, and 9/11 (both of which were abnormal accidents or had strong elements of the abnormal) now rival natural disasters in both their scope and their magnitude. (As one would expect, most major crises have both normal *and* abnormal elements.) To put it mildly, this is a "first" in human history.

It isn't as easy, of course, to prepare for abnormal accidents as it is for normal ones.[3] It is difficult and distasteful to imagine that fellow human beings would want to destroy businesses deliberately, sometimes with the collusion of employees, and might even be willing to kill themselves in the process. This notion threatens to destroy our deeply held beliefs about people, society,

Table 1-1. The differences between normal and abnormal accidents.

Normal	Abnormal
Break Down	Break Up
Omission /Commission	Commission/Omission
Human/ Organizational Error	Human/ Organizational Psychopathology
Systems Complexity/ Failure	Systems Sociopathology
Safe → Unsafe	Good → Evil
Inherent/Interactive Defects/ Weaknesses	Create/Intensify Inherent Defects/Weaknesses
Faulty Design/Maintenance	Exploit Design/Maintenance Weaknesses
Manufacturing Errors/ Weaknesses	Vulnerabilities
Breaches of Security	Penetration of Security
Lack of Intelligent Design	Lack of Just/Compassionate Design
Failure of Expenditures/Controls	Failure of Justice
Passive Neglect	Active Tampering
Unintentional	Intentional
Stupidity	Evil

and business. Thus, companies such as RB are inclined to deny and to disavow the size and the scope of abnormal accidents. Even a year after the World Trade Center was brought down, the vast majority of the executives that my colleagues and I interviewed were not willing to consider the possibility of a similar attack on their offices or factories.[4] The same is true in the after-

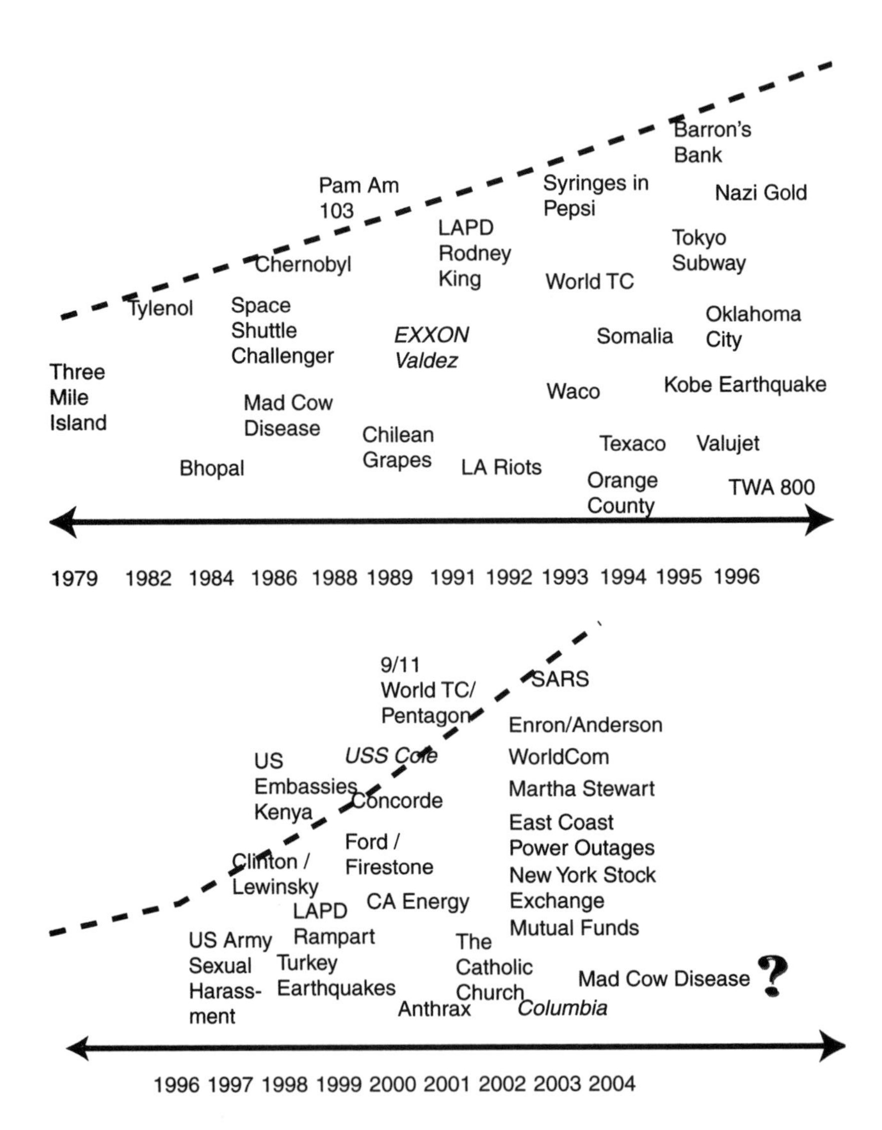

Figure 1-1. A timeline of major crises.

math of Enron and Arthur Andersen—people want to believe that it couldn't happen to them. It not only can, but unfortunately, the probability is very high that it will.

Businesses have no alternative but to think about and prepare for the abnormal. They owe it to us as well. It is estimated that up to 80 percent of all terrorist acts happen to private businesses and not to the government. Thus, business has to do its share if as a society we are to be better prepared to handle the threats posed by terrorism.

If abnormal accidents weren't bad enough, the character of normal accidents has also changed dramatically. This adds another complication to the mix. Twenty years ago, normal accidents were confined mainly to single industries. That is, normal accidents took place mainly *within* a single company or industry. Now, because of the extreme coupling and interdependency of modern societies, normal accidents now occur *between* industries.

The power blackouts that occurred in August 2003 in the Midwest and on the East Coast of the United States are prime illustrations of the changing character of normal accidents. Electricity and information are the twin lifebloods of modern societies.[5] If electricity and information are disrupted, then everything from the production of food, to the supply of potable water, to ATM service—in short, literally everything in a modern society—grinds to a halt. But it also works the other way as well. A major disruption in any part of society now has the ability to affect disruptions in any other part. We are truly coupled and interdependent as never before. Further complicating the situation is the fact that corruptions of the food system and the threat of bioterrorism cut across both the government and private business. If dealing with government and business bureaucracies weren't bad enough, coping with the interfaces between them is even worse. The point is that how society is organized or, better yet, disorganized, is a big part of the problem. It will be a long time before we can say that the entire food system, that is, of producing, packaging, and distributing food, is truly protected against bioterrorism, if ever fully. (As this book was being written, the 9/11 Commission hearings had established that the design and organization of the F.B.I. and C.I.A. were highly dysfunctional, to put it mildly. That is, those forms of organization—or, better yet, disorganization—were severe impediments to getting information with regard to terrorism, let alone doing something about it.)

Leading-Edge Organizations

My colleagues and I have found that there are a small number of leading-edge organizations that have successfully learned how to reduce, but not eliminate entirely, the potential for major crises.[6] They have found ways to lower substantially the probabilities of abnormal accidents, and they have developed the means to contain and lower substantially the economic, human, and existential costs of those crises that still manage to occur. (By existential costs I mean the felt loss of meaning and purpose that is the inevitable outcome of all abnormal accidents. For instance, 9/11 not only had major negative effects on the national economy but also produced widespread feelings of despair, anger, and hopelessness. This was due in part to the fact that the United States was no longer protected by two large oceans. These points are discussed later in this chapter.)

As we shall see, preparing for and protecting against the abnormal or the unthinkable mean acting like a controlled paranoid, but not actually being one (this idea is discussed in depth in Chapter Five). Businesses have to learn to welcome thoughts about the worst that can happen to them, without letting those thoughts interfere with their hopes and aspirations for the best. In the wake of 9/11 and the scandals that have rocked America's largest and most powerful institutions, companies must confront the disturbing question, "How paranoid do we need to be in order to anticipate, plan for, and cope effectively with major crises, and even acts of evil themselves, without in the process becoming totally deranged or evil ourselves?"

Room for Hope

The ultimate message of this book is one of hope, not despair. It shows that there are ways of coping and preparing for major crises despite the fact that it is impossible to prevent all of them. Indeed, if one could fully prevent all crises, then there would be no need to prepare for them. Even more important, however, is the fact that the methods and the ways of thinking that crisis management (CM) teaches us are precisely the skills that are needed for success in the new global economy. Thus, I am not advocating practicing CM entirely for its own sake.

I cannot emphasize too strongly that organizations exist that have found ways to contain and even lower substantially the economic, human, and existential costs of major crises. This finding may be one of the very few bright spots to emerge from the interviews that we have conducted with the senior executives of those companies that were impacted by 9/11.[7] We found that there is a substantial body of organizations that follow a higher ethical calling. The major operating principle that guides these types of organizations, which we term "socially responsible," is: "Do no harm to even a single individual irrespective of the cost of implementing such a policy." As a direct result, these organizations experience one-third fewer total crises than those organizations that do not follow such a principle. (Over a three-year period, responsible organizations experienced on average nine major crises; less responsible organizations experienced sixteen. In other words, less responsible organizations experienced some 44 percent more crises than responsible ones.) Responsible organizations are precisely the ones that are pioneering methods for engaging in controlled paranoia and other new and creative CM strategies.

Less responsible organizations follow the ethical principle: "Do what is right but if and only if it is cost-effective." Interestingly, less responsible organizations, which are primarily interested in maximizing profits, are substantially less profitable (an average of 2 percent return on assets, or ROA) than those organizations that are primarily interested in doing good (on average, 6 percent ROA)! In short, a higher ethical stance literally pays off in fewer crises and greater profits.

More responsible organizations also enjoy a significantly higher standing in *Fortune*'s list of most admired companies. Again, not only does ethics "pay off handsomely" but those companies that embrace a higher moral code do so because "it is the right thing to do, not because it leads to better rewards." But by maintaining ethics for its own sake they become more profitable. They "win" on both accounts.

The Psychological Toll

All crises, but especially abnormal catastrophes, affect us deeply. For this reason, I cannot overemphasize the deep and prolonged psychological impacts of all major crises. Indeed, the psychological aspects are the most important of all the various facets of CM (see Chapter Two). And yet, even though they are so important, the psychological impacts are among the most neglected!

Consider the following: When the two planes crashed into the World Trade Center on September 11, 2001, they not only blew the buildings apart and took the lives of thousands of innocent victims but they also destroyed something equally precious. They shattered some of our most fundamental, most basic, and sacred assumptions about the world. The most basic assumption was that we were safe, secure, and protected from evil. The following is one of the most important expressions of this sentiment:

> More than 30 times in the last seven months, [President George W.] Bush has used variations on a theme to describe the U.S. as vulnerable. . . . He said that before 9/11, "we thought oceans would protect us forever." . . . "The world changed on Sept. 11. . . . In our country, it used to be that oceans could protect us—at least we thought so." . . . But since Pearl Harbor, the oceans have not served as a buffer . . . Why does Bush insist on such rhetoric? "This notion of unprecedented vulnerability is absolutely crucial to the Bush team's anti-constitutional program," says Mark Crispin Miller, author of *The Bush Dyslexicon.* "What that statement really means is, 'We were safe, now we're in danger, and the danger is so severe that you must give me all possible power. What the oceans once did, now only I can do.' "[8]

Oklahoma City: A Prime Example of Shattered Assumptions

Every crisis, no matter how different it is on its surface, violates a common set of assumptions that we have been making about the world, about others, and about ourselves. When these assumptions are shown to be false, our basic social contract with the world is torn apart. The end result is a deep existential crisis that we experience as a fundamental loss of meaning and purpose. We feel betrayed to our very core.

If there is a single, major theme that underlies this book, it is the central role that assumptions play in the construction and management of reality. Assumptions are the bedrock upon which we both construct and manage our world. If our fundamental assumptions are wrong, then everything that is built on them is also wrong. This is why it is so important to bring assumptions to the surface, to analyze and debate our assumptions, especially the more critical that they are.

Deep feelings of betrayal are a significant part of every major crisis that I have studied or about which I have been consulted. The collapse or the invalidation of assumptions *is* one of the major forms of betrayal. Since one of the worst consequences of betrayal is the felt loss of meaning in our lives, a renewed sense of purpose—in its broadest terms, spirituality—becomes essential in restoring that belief, confidence, and faith in the goodness of the world. For this reason, spirituality is an integral component of CM (see Chapter Seven).

One thing is clear. Crises big and small increasingly define who and what we are. Major acts of betrayal and major crises are the common threads. We are in an age of crises and betrayal.

April 19, 1995, began like any other morning. As usual, Jane Brown (not her real name) left her house at 7:15 A.M. At 7:30, she deposited her two children, ages three and five, at the daycare center on the second floor of the Alfred P. Murrah Federal Office Building in Oklahoma City, where Jane worked on the fifth floor. It was a perfect arrangement. Jane could literally pop in and check on her children whenever she wanted. And the children were constantly comforted and reassured by the fact that their mother was always nearby and available.

At precisely 9:03 A.M., Jane and her two children were killed almost instantly as the result of a horrendous explosion. One hundred forty-nine innocent men and women and nineteen children were murdered when a car bomb planted by Timothy McVeigh, an American terrorist, literally tore the building apart. The lives of the surviving families, relatives, and friends were shattered as well.

By now, these facts are of course well known. However, I believe, in the long run, one of the least emphasized aspects of the bombing will prove to be just as important as the physical havoc and destruction. This is the fact—one that I cannot emphasize too much—that the bombing also demolished some of our most basic assumptions about the safety and the security of our nation. As a result, the general mood of the citizens of Oklahoma, and the American public as a whole, was altered dramatically. Our lives were changed forever.

Three Major Assumptions of Oklahoma City

Prior to the bombing, there were three deep assumptions. They were regarded as "basic truths." Just to raise them to the surface for discussion and debate would have been extremely difficult, if not impossible, and yet in a few short seconds they were completely obliterated:

1. By virtue of Oklahoma's location deep in the heartland of America, terrorism will not happen here; terrorism only happens in certain dangerous locations such as Europe and the Middle East; Oklahoma City is protected from the "outside world"; the rest of the world may be dangerous, but Oklahoma is not.

2. An American will not kill other Americans; an American will not commit an act of terrorism against other Americans;

terrorists may be "home grown" in other cultures, but not in ours.

3. Taking the lives of innocent men and women, and especially of young children, is unthinkable; what "crime" could they have possibly committed to justify such a heinous act?

Every major crisis exposes and invalidates similar assumptions. The end result is invariably the same: the overwhelming feeling that we have been fundamentally misled—in effect, betrayed by our own convictions. Suddenly and without warning, the world and our lives no longer make sense. Little wonder, then, that in the case of Oklahoma City, President Clinton and the Reverend Billy Graham came to the site of the bombing to preside over a day of "spiritual healing" for the entire nation. When something so senseless and unprecedented happens on so large a scale, unusual steps must be taken to restore our sense of well-being.

Generic Assumptions

The most generic form of the three assumptions that were shattered by the Oklahoma City bombing is:

1. The world is basically safe and secure; certainly America is safe and protected from attack.

2. Americans are just and ethical; they can be trusted not to kill other Americans.

3. Americans share a common set of values such that the killing of innocent people is literally unthinkable; in other words, when it comes to basic values, all Americans are essentially alike.

Most people are of course neither fully aware nor conscious of these assumptions. They certainly do not voice them directly or in the words that I have used. Nonetheless, from the interviews that I have conducted over the years, it is clear that people feel them deeply in their bones. They feel a deep sense of betrayal when the assumptions, the basic premises, that they have depended upon to function and to make sense of the world no longer work.

I should clarify that this book is not about Oklahoma City or terrorism per se. Oklahoma City and terrorism are just examples of the kinds of major crises we are experiencing on a more frequent basis.

The Most General Set of Assumptions

Similar sets of assumptions, as well as new ones, were further invalidated by 9/11. As a result, the resulting existential crisis penetrated the American psyche even deeper. September 11 disillusionments were exacerbated by the scandals that rocked American corporations and the Catholic Church. Indeed, all of these crises exposed the full and deeper set of basic assumptions that we were making about the world:

1. The world (one's person, organizations, basic institutions, society) is safe and secure.

2. The world is good and just; the unjust will receive appropriate and swift punishment; the guilty will not go free and unpunished.

3. The world is stable and predictable; the ways things are today will be what they are tomorrow; continuity prevails; what is true today will necessarily be true tomorrow; crises are rare aberrations; they are the not the normal state of affairs.

a. The world will return to what it was before—that is, things can be fixed, mended, and repaired; there is reason for hope; beliefs in the continuity, safety, and stability of the world will prevail once again.

4. Crises (damage in general) are limited in scope and magnitude; they are confined to certain persons, organizations, and such; in other words, crises will not cut across all levels of society; not only are there clear boundaries, but they will be respected and maintained; so, for instance, 9/11 clearly violated this assumption. Indeed, 9/11 affected the entire airline industry and the Southern California tourist industry in particular.

5. People are inherently good; they can be trusted to keep their word, promises, and such—that is, they do not have a defective character; in other words, evil is limited.

a. A particularly important variant of this principle is the notion that the world can be divided into us and them—that is, the "good guys" and the "bad guys"; in other words, there is a clear differentiation between us and the Axes of Evil.

6. I am good, competent, and loyal; I am blameless and undeserving of what happened to me; I can trust my own instincts not to betray myself.

a. The crisis was unintentional and not deliberate; it was accidental and unplanned.

b. The perpetrators feel guilt and remorse for their acts.

c. The perpetrators deserve to be forgiven; they are worthy of forgiveness.

7. There were no serious advance warnings that I, my organization, my society was about to experience a major crisis; in other words, there was no way that I could have known about the crisis in advance.

Sadly, virtually all crises follow the same pattern. This is the special sense in which all crises—however much they differ on their surface—are essentially the same. And this is the point for going back and re-examining Oklahoma City, plus many of the other crises that have happened subsequently.

No wonder major crises are so traumatic. One's entire belief system—one's entire set of assumptions—is completely destroyed.

Unless we learn from past crises—history, in general—we are doomed to experience those crises over and over again. If every crisis invalidates the same basic assumptions over and over again, then we need to speed up the recognition of these assumptions, so that it is possible to recover better, sooner, and faster from the growing number of crises that beset and overwhelm us.

Concluding Remarks

The tainting of Tylenol capsules in September 1982, in a suburb outside of Chicago, is generally credited as the beginning of the modern field of CM. (Tylenol capsules laced with cyanide were placed on the shelves in several retail outlets.) McNeil Pharmaceuticals, a subdivision of Johnson & Johnson (J&J), was the manufacturer of Tylenol. By virtue of its quick and responsible actions, J&J is generally credited with being a role model for effective CM. Indeed, even though it was asked not to do so by the FBI, so as not to encourage copycats, J&J voluntarily pulled 7 million bottles of its product off the shelves. Unfortunately, J&J

did not behave as well when, a few years later, Tylenol was implicated in liver damage if one consumed the medication with wine.

The moral of the story is: The fact that an organization has performed well when it is the *victim* of product tampering (i.e., when cyanide was placed in Tylenol) does not guarantee that it will behave well when it is accused of being a *villain.*

However, there is more to the story than this. When J&J responded to the tainting of Tylenol, the modern field of CM had yet to be invented. For this reason alone, it could not have practiced effective or *preventive* CM (see Appendix B). What J&J did do well was to practice effective crisis communications (CC). That is, it communicated effectively with innumerable stakeholders (see Chapter Three) *after* the crisis occurred. But this means that J&J, as well as many other organizations, learned the wrong lesson from the Tylenol episode. They believed, and apparently many still do, that CM is *only* CC. As we shall see, this is far from being even a partial truth.

Notes

1. Charles Perrow, *Normal Accidents: Living with High Risk Technologies* (New York: Basic Books, 1984).
2. See Ian I. Mitroff, *Crisis Leadership: Planning for the Unthinkable* (New York: John Wiley, 2003).
3. Bruce Schneier, *Beyond Fear: Thinking Sensibly About Security in an Uncertain World* (New York: Copernicus Books, 2003).
4. Murat Alpaslan and Ian I. Mitroff, "Bounded Morality: A Study of Crisis Management in the Fortune 1000 Before and After 9/11," unpublished paper, 2004.
5. See The Committee on Science and Technology for Countering Terrorism, A National Research Council of the National Academies, *Making the Nation Safer: The Role of Science and Technology in Countering Terrorism* (Washington, D.C.: The National Academy Press, 2002).

CHAPTER TWO

Challenge 1

Right Heart (Emotional IQ): Deny Denial; Grieve Before a Crisis Occurs

The beleaguered CIA faces new criticism in an internal report submitted this week by [Richard J.] Kerr, [the former Deputy Director] who found serious fault with the agency's analysis on Iraq . . . [Kerr] believed intelligence officers had not come to grips with the causes or scope of the failure.

Kerr's comments were echoed by members of Congress who said they were becoming increasingly impatient with the agency's refusal to acknowledge that its assessments on Iraq were fundamentally flawed.

"They're in denial," said Rep. Jane Harman (D-CA), the ranking Democrat on the House Intelligence Committee. "It's critically important for the national security challenges in the future that these problems get fixed. And I've seen no evidence that they are owning up to it."

—Greg Miller, "Insider Faults CIA on Iraq Analysis,"
Los Angeles Times, January 31, 2004, pp. A1, A8

In 1992, a French Airline company plane crashed on the Saint Odile mountain during . . . landing . . . just before reaching the Strassbourg Airport. Only a dozen people survived the crash. A few months after [the] air crash, I had the opportunity to meet with one of the Vice Presidents. . . . Beyond the technical expla-

nations of [the] catastrophe, his analysis . . . struck me. He considered that the Mont Saint Odile crash was not a crisis. He even explained that he viewed it exactly as the opposite *[italics in original] of a crisis, based on the fact that the morning after the crash the level of the seats reserved in the planes . . . had not moved one iota. This is the perfect illustration of a complete denial of [a] crisis, where people manage major events by ignoring their very existence.*

—Christophe Roux-Dufort, "Why Organizations Don't Learn from Crises: The Perverse Power of Normalization," *Review of Business*, Fall 2000, p. 25

Many organizations apportion blame by seeking out scapegoats [read: villains] for the cause of adverse events. This search for culpability can actually make subsequent failure more likely as individuals [read: potential victims] become reluctant to raise warnings about impending problems, or cover-up issues. Invariably, this will severely hinder the potential for effective communication, cultural change, and, in turn, learning. In such a setting of non trust, key managers and operators may not only contain potentially damaging information but may reconstruct their accounts of events to protect themselves from blame.

—Dominic Elliott, Denis Smith, and Martina McGuinness, "Exploring the Failure to Learn: Crises and the Barriers to Learning," *Review of Business*, Fall 2000, p. 18

The Argument

1. Emotional preparation for crises is the most difficult and the most important preparation of all; get beyond denial; confront it straight on.
2. Before one can work on crises, one has to spend the time and energy working on oneself. If one is not prepared emotionally, then valuable time and energy will be lost in working on the crises themselves.
3. Operate on the assumption that the worst not only can but will happen to you and to your family, organization, society; don't waste your time and energy asking why it happened.
4. Crises are equal opportunity events; they happen to everyone.
5. You can and will survive—even prosper—but if, and only if, you are prepared emotionally, physically, intellectually, and spiritually.
6. Hire counselors to work through the powerful emotions associated with all crises *before* they occur; get the grieving over so that you can get back to living sooner and more fully.
7. Accept the painful fact that the abnormal—that is, intentionally evil acts such as 9/11—has become the new normal state of affairs.
8. Accept the fact that in today's unrelenting 24/7/365 media-saturated world, there are no secrets anymore; the media can find out anything they want to about

anyone, any corporation, and so on; secret documents and private conversations are exposed regularly on the 6 P.M. news and the front pages of major newspapers; if you do not accept this, then you will suffer an additional crisis—that is, the shock that comes from having all of one's personal and company secrets paraded before the public for all to see.

9. Abide by the principle, "If you deny and lie, then you will be tried and fried in the court of public opinion; you will not only be hung out to dry, but to die."
10. Understand that if you are in any way guilty regarding the cause of the crisis, or if you failed to prepare adequately for it, then you will be perceived as the villain; your own employees, the public, and others will perceive that you have betrayed them.
11. In the end, all crises are perceived and experienced as major acts of betrayal so that if the original crisis was not bad enough, the subsequent feelings of betrayal will be even worse.

In Chapter One, we briefly met Mary Douglas, CEO of Rural Books (RB). We learned that neither she nor her top executives were prepared for the crisis that occurred. To understand why this was the case, let us flash back in time to about a year before the crisis happened.

Mary was chairing the regular monthly meeting of her top

executive team. The heads of Legal, Marketing, Finance, Production, Acquisitions, Information Technology, Human Resources, and Public Affairs were there as permanent, standing members. So was Robert Turnbull, Senior Executive V.P. and RB's Chief Operating Officer, whom we also encountered very briefly in Chapter One. In addition, Bob Hunt, Head of Risk Management and Security, was there as a special invited guest. In contrast to the other members, he was not a permanent member of the Executive Team.

Bob was invited to deliver a special report that he had prepared on the major risks facing RB. His report showed in no uncertain terms that the most probable and the most costly risks facing RB were fire and water damage due to spring floods caused by melting snow. Either risk could do extensive damage to RB's production facilities and its raw materials, mostly paper. RB's situation was complicated by the fact that normally what could inhibit and extinguish fires—for example, water—could also do considerable damage to RB's basic raw materials. Additionally, water could do extensive damage to RB's expensive production computers and graphic equipment. Therefore, Bob recommended the installation of special fire-inhibiting foam and paneling throughout RB's facilities. He also recommended the installation of special fire-retardant walls that would likewise prevent damage to RB's computers and graphic equipment. Sprinklers would be used, but only if they were needed to save lives. With little fanfare, the Executive Committee quickly and unanimously approved the expenditure of $250,000 to protect and upgrade RB's facilities.

The second part of Bob's report was, unfortunately, not as well received. It was, in fact, received quite negatively. Bob informed the committee that he recently had attended a three-day special course on crisis management (CM). Without going into all of the details, he explained that CM took a much broader view of risks than traditional risk management (RM). (See Appendix B for a brief primer on CM and the differences between crisis management, risk management, and crisis communications.)

RM typically ranks risks according to their consequences, multiplied by their probabilities of occurrence. According to this procedure, the risks that one should prepare for were precisely those that had high consequences should they occur (e.g., high injuries or high costs) and simultaneously high probabilities of occurring. Fires and water damage were in fact the highest ranked risks according to this procedure.

Indeed, the procedure of multiplying the severity of a risk times its probability of occurrence has the general effect of selecting high-consequence, high-probability events for attention. In fact, high-consequence but low-probability events are almost guaranteed to be neglected—that is, not to be considered at all.

Of course, in order to perform RM, one has to have some way of estimating both the consequences and the probabilities of the occurrence of potential risks. Usually this is done through studying historical records—that is, the frequency with which past, known events, or risks have occurred.

Once again, according to RM, the risks that one should prepare for are precisely those that have high consequences (e.g., high injuries or high costs) and simultaneously high probabilities of their occurring. However, Bob also noted that the course had made him aware that there was a whole other category or type of risks that all businesses should consider, but unfortunately rarely did. These were high-consequence, low-probability risks. The premiere example was 9/11. Obviously, terrorist acts directed against skyscrapers, especially in New York City and Washington, D.C., were high-consequence crises. But at the same time, they were judged to be of low probability, even though the intelligence and risk communities had for years suggested strongly that such events should be considered more likely. While perhaps unlikely, they were not impossible, and therefore, not completely improbable. Indeed, the intelligence and risk communities argued that there were strong reasons to believe that the probabilities of their occurrence were actually increasing.

To demonstrate why one needed to consider such events, the instructor pointed out that prior to 9/11 the most likely scenario for bringing down a high rise was that of placing a bomb inside the building by means of a suitcase. Flying a plane into a building was considered so improbable as to not even be worth considering. And yet it was precisely such an event that needed to be considered because most people didn't want to consider it!

Closer to home, Bob suggested that RB ought to brainstorm how other types of crises—for instance, product tampering—might apply to their business. Unfortunately, because Bob could not suggest any specific examples of product tampering that might apply to RB, his proposal fell on deaf ears. Mary politely but firmly led the charge: "Bob, I believe that I speak for all of us when I say how much we appreciate all of your efforts to protect RB. But, frankly, this is highly speculative. I can't imagine in my wildest dreams how RB could ever be the object of terrorists. We're not big or important enough. We're certainly not in a major metropolitan area. If anything, we're on the fringes. Terrorism, except maybe for ecoterrorism, just doesn't happen around here. As for product tampering, that is equally unlikely. I can't imagine any kind of a scenario where anybody would want to tamper with our products. I think that you need to confine your efforts to the protection of RB's physical assets and our employees."

In order to understand Mary's reasoning, as well as that of

the other members of the executive team, it is important to appreciate that every one of them was imaginative and highly creative. Indeed, it took a great deal of imagination and considerable risk to open RB in the first place.

While Mary had grown up in Montana, she had gone to an elite Eastern school for her undergraduate degree in math and history. She had also attended another elite Eastern university for her MBA, where she majored in corporate finance. It took a lot of guts to open RB. More than once and with great relish, Mary recounted the story of how she had received a C in her MBA class in Business Strategy, where she first proposed the concept of RB. She had received a C because the idea was too outlandish. And yet, barely ten years after its founding, RB was an enormous financial success. Mary had successfully foreseen and capitalized on the huge demand and desire for natural, organic foods that was soon to develop and to take hold nationwide.

Normal Versus Abnormal Business

To understand why Mary and her top team were not prepared for the crisis that struck RB, one needs to understand that the qualities that make for success in running a business in normal times are not the same qualities that make for success in managing a major crisis, certainly not in abnormal times. Normal business demands for the most part that we learn to recognize and to manage stress. Crises, on the other hand, demand that we confront and overcome some of humankind's deepest and darkest feelings. These are the emotions that are connected with denial, fear, betrayal, and the exposure to severely traumatic situations. To manage these kinds of feelings and emotions, one needs to develop a capacity for resilience.[1] In turn, this necessitates that Mary and her top executive team undergo a rigorous and systematic program of *pre-crisis* psychological training. They need to take both a personal and an organizational audit of their psychological capacities to confront and to survive major crises.

The purpose of pre-crisis psychological training is not to be anxiety or worry free. No such things are possible. The purpose is to be better able to assess and to manage the anxieties that accompany all crises. In other words, the purpose is not to be overwhelmed by fear or anxiety, but to be better able to cope with them.

Denial

One of the earliest and one the most important discoveries made by Sigmund Freud was the existence and the operation of defense mechanisms.[2] Because the ego of a young child is so fragile—it can easily be overwhelmed by all kinds of primitive fears and fantasies—the tiny amount of consciousness that the child has developed within a few months of its separation from its mother is always in danger of falling back into a state of unconsciousness—that is, a state of primitive fusion union with the mother. In other words, the child is in danger of regressing to a more primitive and earlier state of development—that is, being engulfed by the mother. Defense mechanisms are nature's extraordinarily clever way of protecting the fragile ego of the child from threats to its existence. Table 2-1 lists the major defense mechanisms discovered by Freud and his colleagues. These are shown in the left-hand column. The right-hand column shows some of the typical forms that these mechanisms take in organizations.

It is one thing for defense mechanisms to be used by young children to protect their fragile and developing egos or minds. It is quite another for these same mechanisms to be used to protect supposedly mature adults and organizations from thinking about

Table 2-1. Defense mechanisms.

Types of Defense Mechanisms	Examples
Denial	Crises only happen to others. We are invulnerable.
Disavowal	Crises happen, but their impact on our organization is small.
Idealization	Crises do not happen to good organizations in out-of-the-way places.
Grandiosity	We are so big and powerful that we will be protected from crises and we can handle anything that is thrown our way.
Projection	If a crisis happens, then it must be because someone else is bad or out to get us.
Intellectualization	We don't have to worry about crises since the probabilities of their occurrence are too small. Before a crisis can be taken seriously, one would have to measure precisely its odds of occurrence and its consequences.
Compartmentalization	Crises cannot affect our whole organization since the parts are independent of one another.

unpleasant things that need to be confronted. It is also bad enough to hear denial expressed by a single person in an organization. It is quite another to hear it voiced by a majority of the members of an organization. That is truly scary. When this happens, the denial is collective, and for this reason it is much harder to confront and to root out.

We have already seen the first defense mechanism—denial—at work in Mary's response to Bob. Mary denied outright that terrorism and product tampering were even remote possibilities. Mary also used disavowal and idealization when she argued that RB was in an out-of-the-way place. She also used them when she argued that RB was not big and important enough to warrant preparation for certain kinds of crises. Thus, unconsciously she diminished the potential size and the importance of a particular set of crises.

The fact that no one really challenged Mary is also evidence for the fact that there was a kind of collusion or unconscious buy-in by the group.[3] This is not to say that under their breath no one disagreed with Mary. Rather, no one raised objections to the level of public discourse and disagreement. In this sense, there was collusion by the members of the group not to disagree openly either with one another or with their superiors. (We shall also discuss the phenomenon of denial in Chapter Five as well. Unfortunately, denial is widespread. For example, a few years ago, my colleagues and I audited a worldwide organization that served disadvantaged children around the globe. We audited the organization for potential crises that it could face. In conducting our interviews, the possibility of pedophilia surfaced more than once. However, when we brought this to the attention of those at the headquarters of the organization, pedophilia was dismissed out of hand as not a possibility at all.)

Trauma

While certainly not all crises are equally traumatic or traumatizing, all crises have the potential to be traumatic. The major difference between denial and trauma is as follows: denial involves denying the unpleasant feelings associated with potentially traumatic events *before* they occur. In contrast, trauma involves the denial of feelings *after* a traumatic event has occurred.

Denial protects *before* a traumatic event whereas what we call a "traumatic reaction" involves the denial of painful feelings and emotions *after* a traumatic event has occurred. In the case of denial, the mind shuts down *before* a crisis happens, whereas *in reaction to* a traumatic event, the mind shuts down *after* it has occurred. In either case, the feelings, the fears, and the emotions surrounding a potential or an already experienced crisis are too painful for the conscious mind to accept. Thus, in the case of denial, the mind prepares by denying the event—that is, the painful feelings, fears, and emotions that are associated with it. In contrast, the reactions to a traumatic event involve the mind's shutting down after the event has occurred in order to protect the mind from further damage by reliving painful events.

Both cases involve the numbing or the diminishing of the strong emotions that are associated with crises, real and potential. Both of these reactions are not entirely negative. They have certain beneficial effects. For instance, one of the most painful emotions associated with traumatic events is guilt. After 9/11, many of the survivors asked, "Why did I survive when my best friends died?"

The feelings of guilt associated with being a survivor are often so painful that in order to spare oneself, the mind doesn't merely go numb but shuts down entirely. This shutting-down process is never complete or successful. This is why Vietnam Vets and others who have survived traumatic events often experience flashbacks and nightmares months, and even years, after the event. They also are more prone to prolonged bouts of depression.

Forgetting is never perfect or complete. For this reason alone, it is strongly recommended that those who have experienced traumatic events be seen by experienced, trained counselors within 24 hours of the event. If a person delays for even a day in getting to a trained counselor or therapist, then he or she is likely to go into posttraumatic denial.

Betrayal

One of the most striking and interesting features of crises is that, virtually without exception, they are experienced as major acts of betrayal. And yet paradoxically, this is one of the least studied and least discussed aspects of crises. For this reason, I want to discuss not only the phenomenon of betrayal but especially how it pertains to RB and the crisis it is facing. In all likelihood, Mary and her top team will be viewed as villains—that is, as having betrayed their employees, the surrounding community, and their customers— because they had not thought about the particular crisis that RB experienced and hence were not adequately prepared for it.

If RB's crisis is like those that have assumed prominence in recent years—for example, Ford-Firestone, the Catholic Church, WorldCom—then near-verbatim minutes of the CM Team meeting where product tampering was first proposed will somehow be obtained, most likely from a disgruntled employee. It will then be shown as one of the lead stories on all of the major news networks. As a result, Mary and her top management team will be blamed for not having done more to protect its consumers. In short, Mary and RB will be vilified even though there may have been very little, if anything, that they could have done to have prevented the crisis.

Crises are generally experienced as major acts of betrayal because people need to have someone to blame for the crisis. Unfortunately, blaming is a central feature of virtually all major crises. It is one of the principal ways in which we cope with the strong feelings and emotions that crises stir up.

A Working Definition of Betrayal

Betrayal is the failure of a person, an organization, an institution, or a society to act and to behave in accordance with ways that they have promised or they have led us to believe that they will. Betrayal is the violation of the trust that we have placed in another person, organization, institution, and/or society. Thus, betrayal is profoundly rooted in our basic feelings of trust and goodness with regard to others.

The greater the expectation that a person will act and behave in the ways that were promised, and the greater the consequences (seriousness) of their not doing so, then the greater the felt sense of betrayal. Sometimes the promise is stated explicitly; most of the time, it is unstated and implicit. It is implied and taken for granted.

Some acts of betrayal are conscious and deliberate. In such cases, the betrayer calculates brazenly whether betrayal is in his or her best interests. If the "benefits" exceed the "costs," then betrayal is "worth it." If the "costs" exceed the "benefits," then it is not.

Most acts of betrayal are unintentional. They are an unintended consequence of an act or behavior. Often, the person committing the act is completely unaware or unconscious of what he or she has done. By the same token, most people who betray someone else experience guilt; very few do not. Those who do not experience guilt are the really scary ones. They are also the most dangerous. They are psycho- and sociopaths.

In the case of Enron, there are strong reasons to believe that the top executives were in effect *behaving* like sociopaths.[4] (Whether they were in fact sociopaths is of course another matter.) For instance, they exhibited little or no feelings of guilt or remorse for their behavior or actions. Even worse, there are strong reasons to believe that Enron exhibited the characteristics of a sociopathic organization. Worst of all is the fear that we have created a society that fosters and rewards sociopathic behavior. In effect, we have created a dangerous "variant" of capitalism—sociopathic capitalism!

In every case, betrayal is the violation of a basic and fundamental assumption we are making about an individual, an organization, an institution, or society—for example, that another person will stand up for us, act in our best interests, and protect us. When the assumption—or more commonly, a set of assumptions—has been shown to be false or invalid, as in Oklahoma City and 9/11, we are stunned. We are left with the feeling of having been betrayed to our core.

For over twenty-five years, I have been studying how people and organizations react to crises. The following is a typical response. It shows the explicit and the strong connection between crises and betrayal:

> As bad as the crisis was that our organization experienced, even worse was the feeling that we had been betrayed by our CEO and top executives. Time and time again, they reassured us that there was no real need to even think about let alone prepare for crises that had already struck the other members of our very own industry. To do so was a needless waste of time, money, and energy.
>
> After all, they argued, since the crises had already occurred, and to someone else, therefore, the probability of their occurring again was even smaller. In retrospect, we were playing a perverse form of Russian roulette. The more that one held a loaded gun to one's head, pulled the trigger, and it didn't fire, the lower the odds were that it would fire the next time, if ever! What nonsense! I should have known better. In this sense, I guess I blame myself as well since I was all too eager to go along.

> The rationale was that by not preparing for crises, we were going to be even more profitable. Of course, it turned out to be the exact opposite. We ended up losing far more money than if we had prepared. The amount of money that we would have spent on preparation would have been a tiny fraction of the cost of the entire crisis.
>
> The fact that I bought into the CEO's assumptions without challenging them was one of the worst things about the entire episode. Maybe it was because I wanted to believe them as well.
>
> What you are left with is the sickening feeling that you can't trust your own judgment. You feel that you have betrayed your own self. What could be worse than this?

Who Betrays Us the Most?

The feelings of being betrayed by a crisis are basically a result of the feelings that the CEO and top management should have taken better care of us. One of the most interesting aspects of crises is that they generally cause people to regress. In effect, the leaders of the organization become the parents, and in turn, everyone else becomes the children. These feelings are intensified by the fact that on a day-in-and-day-out basis, the persons who betray us the most often and the most regularly are our bosses, our immediate co-workers, and our subordinates. The boss is thus already in danger of being the bad parent.

Table 2-2 shows how being betrayed by one's boss as the result of a major crisis results in the collapse of the major assumptions we introduced in Chapter One. That is, as the result of a major crisis, some of the most basic and general assumptions that we have been making about our leaders are invalidated. This

Table 2-2. Basic assumptions that result from being betrayed by one's boss.
1. You, the parent (the boss), *failed* to make the world safe.
2. You, the parent (the boss), *failed* to make the world good and just.
3. You, the parent (the boss), *failed* to make the world stable and predictable; as the result of your failures, things will never be the same again; a. One's world will *never* return to what it was before.
4. You, the parent (the boss), *failed* to make the crisis limited; therefore, you laid the foundation for mistrusting all leaders in organizations in the future.
5. You, the parent (the boss), *failed* to be inherently good.
6. You, the parent (the boss), *failed* to make me good.
7. You, the parent (the boss), *failed* to make it known that I was about to be betrayed by your actions/inactions.

is why a major crisis is often so traumatic. In effect, it violates *all* of the tenets of our basic belief system.

Despite this, nearly all of the people that I have interviewed react to betrayal and to crises by merely "shrugging them off" or by "gutting it through." If they discussed the betrayal or the crisis with anyone else, then it was with a close friend or spouse. The difficulty, of course, occurred when it was the close friend or spouse who was the betrayer. Nonetheless, most people do not seek treatment for any sort of betrayal or crisis.

The Effects of Betrayal: How We View Ourselves Versus How We View Our Betrayers

One of the most striking features of betrayal, especially as it pertains to crises, is how people who have been betrayed view themselves in comparison and in contrast to those who have betrayed them (see Table 2-3 and Figure 2-1). In general, the person, organization, or society that has been betrayed—the victim—views himself, herself, or itself as optimistic, positive, generally upbeat, trusting, easygoing, calm, able to express one's feelings, cheerful, forgiving, happy, hopeful, warm, and reflective. On the other hand, one's betrayer—the villain—is generally viewed as pessimistic, bitter, less upbeat, distrustful, moody, anxious, hiding one's feelings, sour, unforgiving, less happy, hopeless, cold, and unreflective. This contrast is even more striking if we line up the two portraits side by side.

If people are allowed to express their perceptions on a seven-point scale, where, for instance, the number 1 represents a

Table 2-3. The betrayed versus the betrayer.

The Person Betrayed—The Victim	The Betrayer—The Villain
Optimistic	Pessimistic
Positive	Bitter
Generally upbeat	Less upbeat
Trusting	Distrustful
Easygoing	Moody
Calm	Anxious
Able to express one's feelings	Hiding one's feelings
Cheerful	Sour
Forgiving	Unforgiving
Happy	Less happy
Hopeful	Hopeless
Warm	Cold
Reflective	Unreflective

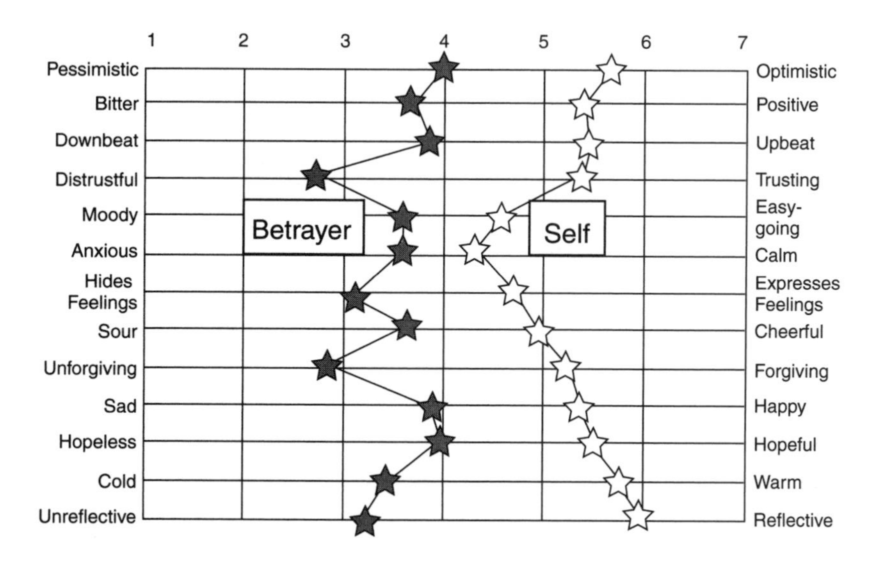

Figure 2-1. Splitting/demonizing.

"marked degree of pessimism," and 7 represents a "marked degree of optimism," then we can compare the two portraits numerically (see Figure 2-2). There is a highly significant statistical difference between the "degree of optimism" that those who have been betrayed feel is characteristic of themselves and the "degree of pessimism" that they feel is characteristic of their betrayer. From a statistical standpoint, the differences between the two perceptions or profiles are so far apart that it is highly unlikely that they are due to chance alone. In other words, we are looking at extreme portraits. These differences can be summarized compactly as follows:

We demonize those who have betrayed us. This is true whether the betrayer is a single individual, an organization, a society, or even a civilization!

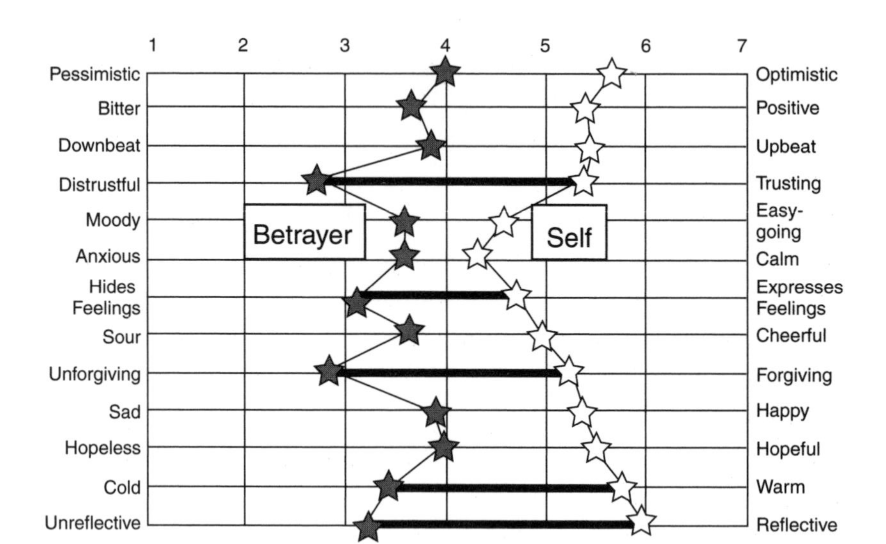

Figure 2-2. The cold-blooded betrayer.

Demonization is one of the most important themes of this book. No matter what the particular type of crisis with which we are dealing, demonization rears its ugly head again and again. Someone or something is always demonized as a result of a major crisis. In fact, this is one of the ways of determining whether something is a "major crisis" or not. If someone or something is being demonized, then there either is, has been, or is about to be a major crisis. In this regard, I need to stress that the perceptions of the "betrayer" are generally the same whether the betrayer is a single individual, an entire organization, a society, or even a civilization. In every case, the profile of the betrayer is essentially the same.

Figure 2-2 helps us to understand the process of demonization even more clearly. Look at the particular scales where the greatest differences occur between the perceptions of oneself as victim and our perceptions of those who have betrayed us. The betrayer is viewed as distrustful, hiding his or her feelings, of being unforgiving, cold, and unreflective. The portrait is one of a "completely cold-blooded person." This helps us to understand why it is so difficult to forgive those who have betrayed us, and no less, to accept amends from them. This also helps to explain why the effects of crises are so long-lasting and extremely difficult to overcome.

Splitting and Compartmentalization

The findings of the previous section are even more general. They pertain to psychological processes that go far beyond betrayal. They are the result of defense mechanisms known as splitting or compartmentalization (see Table 2-1). While important, a detailed discussion of splitting and compartmentalization would take us somewhat afield. Suffice it to say that the portraits between oneself and one's betrayer are severely "split."

Recovering from Crises

This chapter has given us a deeper understanding of what crises do to us, what it takes to recover from them, why they are often so traumatic, and why their effects are so long-lasting. To my knowledge, the link between crises and deep, prolonged feelings of betrayal has not been made explicit before.

To recover from a major crisis, one has to go back, to rebuild, and to readjust the perceptions of those that one feels are responsible for causing the crisis in the first place. For instance, this means that one has to shift the perception of one's "betrayer" or the "villain," from "cold" to "warm." In other words, one has to "re-humanize" the dehumanization that has taken place with regard to one's betrayer, whether an individual, an organization, a society, or even a whole civilization, as in the case of 9/11. Little wonder why this is so difficult to accomplish. Even in the case where the betrayer, villain, or guilty party has accepted responsibility for his or her actions, has admitted it openly, and has even tried to make amends, it is still very difficult to accomplish this change in perception.

Concluding Remarks

The person who, entirely on his or her own, can sort out all of the issues that have been raised in this chapter is rare, indeed. Rare also is the person who can form an accurate portrait of him or herself, let alone of those whom the individual feels been the betrayers in the crisis.

I have no doubt whatsoever that the scores of people I have interviewed and surveyed over the years feel absolutely certain that their profile is "good" (see Figure 2-1)—that is, that they have been victimized. I have no doubt that they feel that those who have betrayed them have the exact opposite profile—that is, that of a villain. Nonetheless, in order for healing to take place, and in general for forgiveness to result, there is no alternative but to adjust the portraits we have of ourselves and that of others.

We have to come to realize and to accept that those who have betrayed us, often unintentionally, have merely become "convenient psychological receptacles" onto which we can project (see Table 2-3) those aspects of ourselves that we do not like, and therefore, do not wish to acknowledge. Thus, as "real" as the portraits are of those who have betrayed us, or caused crises for us, they also represent our unacknowledged sides.

Therapy is one of the few remedies that help to make the world, the betrayer, and the person betrayed whole and safe again.

Of course, ideally, it would be eminently desirable if Mary and her top management team had been aware of all these forces and factors before the crisis. In addition to their training in finance and business, Mary and her top team needed to have had schooling in the psychological impacts of crises. Without such training, they merely react, and in most cases, poorly, to highly emotional, stressful, and traumatic situations.

If the initial crisis that Mary and RB were facing wasn't bad enough, then it will be compounded by all of the powerful feelings that will be unleashed in Mary, her team, in RB's employees, and in all of RB's innumerable other stakeholders as well. Unfortunately, Mary and her top team will most likely be blamed for the crisis, for their not having done more to have foreseen it, even if they couldn't have prevented it. If only for this reason, pre-crisis trauma and psychological training is absolutely essential.

For these reasons, I recommend strongly that every organization call in consultants that are experts in trauma and the psychological effects of crises. Such experts are invaluable in creating realistic simulations that will give people a feel for the strong emotions that they will experience as the result of a crisis.

Undoubtedly, this chapter will seem overly psychological to many readers. For this reason, I cannot stress too much that, psychological or not, it is an accurate description of what happens in the heat of a crisis. The world is managed by people, not machines or impersonal mechanisms. People do not behave as machines during the midst of a crisis.

Once an individual or an organization is in a crisis, then forces are set in motion that are akin to a death spiral, especially if one is not prepared for them. If an individual or an organization is not prepared, it will lose valuable time and energy in treating its own psychological wounds instead of responding to the wounds of others.

From my experience, the psychological factors are without a doubt among the most important, if not *the* most important, in how an individual, an organization, or an entire society responds to a major crisis. One cannot overemphasize the psychological effects of major crises. To de-emphasize and to neglect them is merely another example and form of denial.

From the perspective of this chapter, as important as they are, risk management and business continuity planning are sophisticated forms of denial! They do not go far enough in anticipating and planning for a broad array of crises. They give one false security. They contribute to the illusion that crises and their effects are limited.

Crisis leaders learn one of the most valuable lessons of all: *the fact that one is beyond denial does not mean that everyone else in the organization is*. They have also learned: *do not become paralyzed by your fears and those of others.* Indeed, give people time and space to vent and to work through their fears and anxieties. Above all, never dismiss them; this only makes the fears and anxieties worse.

Notes

1. Karen Reivich and Andrew Shatte, *The Resilience Factor* (New York: Broadway Books, 2002).
2. Yannis Gabriel, *Organizations in Depth* (Thousand Oaks, Calif.: Sage Publications, 1999); see also George Vallant, *Ego Mechanisms of Defense: A Guide for Clinicians and Researchers* (Washington, D.C.: American Psychiatric Press, 1992).
3. Gabriel, *Organizations in Depth.*
4. Brian Cruver, *Anatomy of Greed: The Unshredded Truth from an Enron Insider* (New York: Carroll & Graf, 2002); see also Peter C. Fusaro and Ross Miller, *What Went Wrong at Enron: Everyone's Guide to the Largest Bankruptcy in U.S. History* (New York: John Wiley, 2002).

CHAPTER THREE

Challenge 2
Right Thinking (Creative IQ): Be a Responsible Troublemaker

Challenge 3
Right Social and Political Skills (Social and Political IQ): Be Patiently Impatient

Two UCLA employees have been placed on leave amid a criminal investigation into allegations that they stole body parts from cadavers donated to the medical school and sold them for personal gain, school officials and others familiar with the investigation said Friday.

People familiar with the case said it probably involved dozens of cadavers donated to the school's Willed Body Program over a period of five years. If so, it would dwarf previous scandals involving the sale of cadaver parts at other medical centers around the country.

—Charles Ornstein, "Sale of Body Parts at UCLA Alleged," *Los Angeles Times*, March 6, 2004, p. A1

An Ohio woman was served a salad containing part of a restaurant worker's thumb sliced off while chopping lettuce, a health official said Friday.

The woman "thought it was gristle or something like that" when she tried to chew the uninspected garnish, said William Franks, Health Commissioner for Spark County [Ohio], where the incident occurred earlier this week.

"Physically I think she's OK, other than hysteria" Franks added.

—Times Wire Services, "Diner Gets Salad with Thumb Part," *Los Angeles Times*, March 6, 2004, p. A13

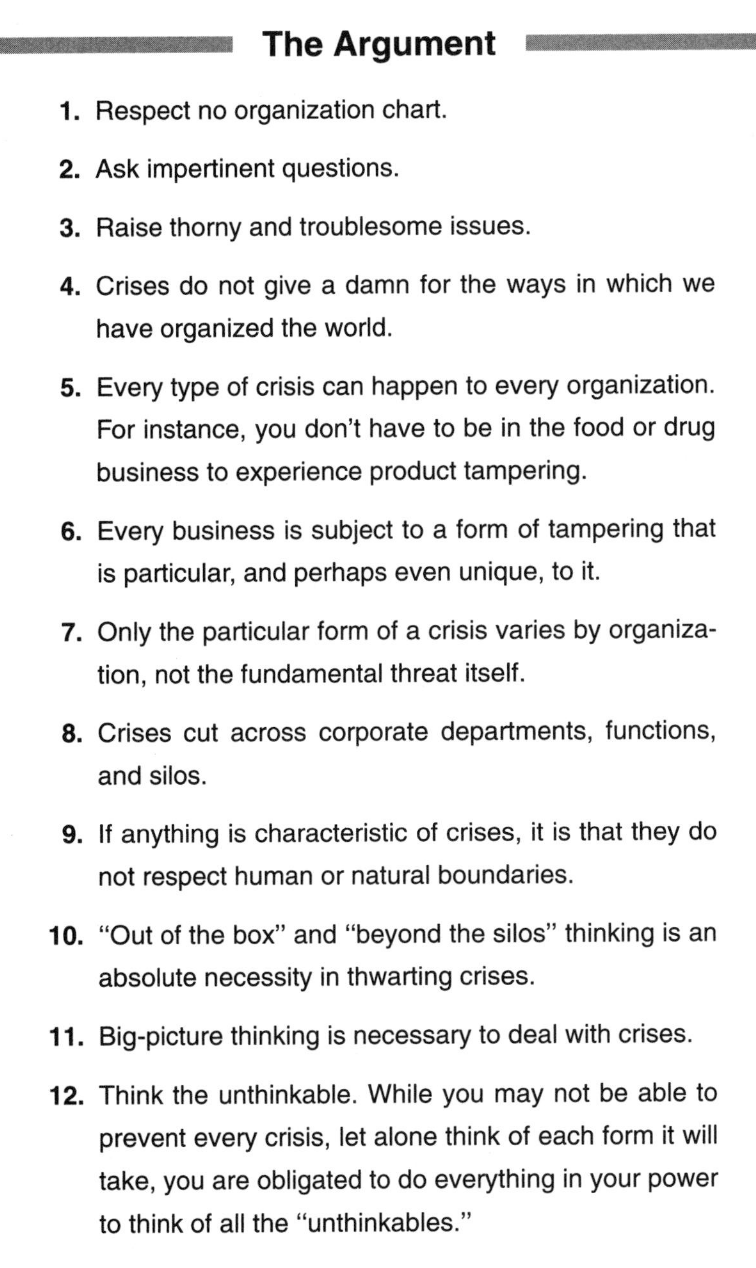

The Argument

1. Respect no organization chart.
2. Ask impertinent questions.
3. Raise thorny and troublesome issues.
4. Crises do not give a damn for the ways in which we have organized the world.
5. Every type of crisis can happen to every organization. For instance, you don't have to be in the food or drug business to experience product tampering.
6. Every business is subject to a form of tampering that is particular, and perhaps even unique, to it.
7. Only the particular form of a crisis varies by organization, not the fundamental threat itself.
8. Crises cut across corporate departments, functions, and silos.
9. If anything is characteristic of crises, it is that they do not respect human or natural boundaries.
10. "Out of the box" and "beyond the silos" thinking is an absolute necessity in thwarting crises.
11. Big-picture thinking is necessary to deal with crises.
12. Think the unthinkable. While you may not be able to prevent every crisis, let alone think of each form it will take, you are obligated to do everything in your power to think of all the "unthinkables."
13. Expect the unexpected.

14. Advance/retreat—that is, go slow, steadily.
15. Gently confront by not confronting.
16. Accept and respect people's fears and anxieties, but do not become enmeshed in them.

When Tom Peters and Robert Waterman published their business bestseller *In Search of Excellence*, one of the key principles they proposed that supposedly distinguished excellent from not so excellent companies was that the former "stuck to their knitting."[1] Excellent companies not only knew what their main businesses were but they also adhered to them religiously. They didn't wander away from their core businesses because they knew their boundaries and limits. Nonetheless, the supposed strength of excellent companies is one of their major limitations, especially when it comes to preparing for and responding to crises. (Besides, many of the so-called excellent companies that Peters and Waterman cited vanished very quickly from their initial list.)

One of the most troubling aspects of major crises is that they "unravel the knitting." Crises are crises precisely because they don't abide by the narrow and artificial boundaries that we have created for ourselves and the world. There is no question that humans need limits in order to make sense of and manage the endlessly complex and confusing world they have created. However, there is no reason to expect that the larger world will respect those boundaries.[2] The "key principles" that are suitable for running your ordinary world and ordinary business are not the same principles that will get you through a major crisis.

Once again we see where crises attack our underlying assumptions: because we believe that the world is bounded, the world thereby conforms to our assumption! As much as companies desire to "stick to their knitting," in today's world all businesses are in all other businesses all of the time! For another, all crises are in all other crises all of the time! These startling propositions are two of the major themes of this chapter.

We need to "unbound" the pictures that we have created. This is precisely what responsible troublemakers do very carefully—that is, in stages, over time. For instance, in order to accomplish this "unbounding" for our example company, Rural Books (RB), Bob Hunt would have had to have understood RB's business(es) better than Mary or her top team did.

All Businesses Are in All Businesses

To show that all businesses are in all other businesses, let us examine the case of RB in more detail. Figure 3-1 presents an overly simplified, if not simplistic, view of RB. It represents the book production business as a basic manufacturing system—namely, one starts with raw materials (paper), binds them into a book, and produces a finished product. (To say that this figure leaves out a few details of production is putting it mildly.) A more realistic view of RB is given in Figure 3-2; however, even this diagram is simplified.

Figure 3-2 starts in the upper left-hand corner with either the active recruitment of prospective authors by RB or with their

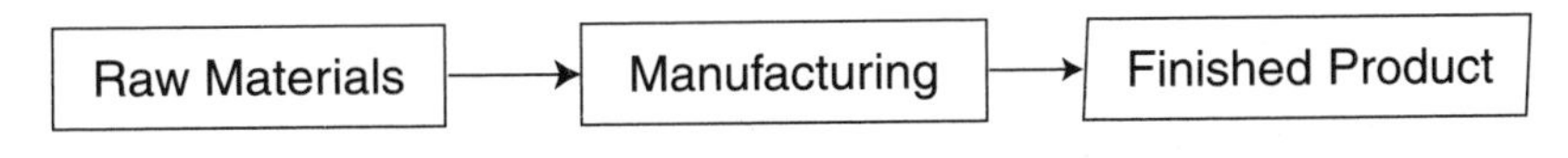

Figure 3-1. A simplifed view of Rural Books (RB).

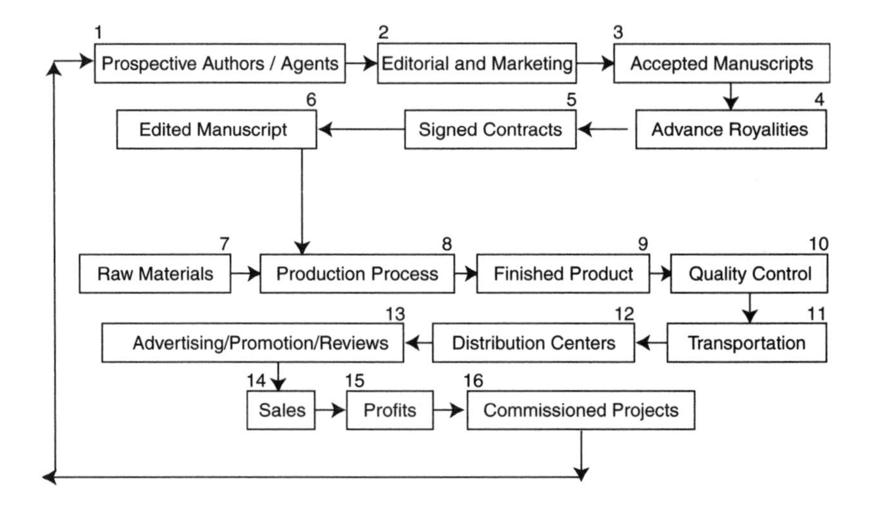

Figure 3-2. A more realistic view of RB.

being brought to the attention of RB via agents who represent prospective authors. Of course, this already presupposes the prior step of the existence of RB itself, as well as RB's having a business plan—that is, the manuscripts and authors it desires to publish. The second box shows that all authors have to go through an editorial and marketing process during which the publisher judges the acceptability of the proposal or manuscript. If the manuscript is deemed acceptable, then the work is accepted for publication. The fourth box indicates that negotiations take place to determine the size of an advance that is acceptable to both the author and RB. (Most publishers offer a monetary advance against royalties in order to secure desirable authors. This advance payment is made before the book is sold and is based on its projected sales.) If the advance is acceptable to both parties, then a contract is signed. Typically, the author gets half of the advance at signing and the remainder when the completed manuscript is accepted. Box 6 represents the editing process. No author, regardless of how talented he or she is, can write a manuscript without some input from a professional editor. An editor reviews the manuscript for clarity without changing the author's style.

Box 7 indicates that raw materials, which have to be procured and therefore require a procurement system, are themselves a major input into the process. To put it mildly, paper—while absolutely necessary—is hardly the single ingredient in publishing, since without an accepted manuscript the production process would have nothing to produce. Box 9 indicates the production of the finished product, namely a book. Box 10, which is especially critical in RB's case, is the process of quality control—that is, quality control is not an "output" or a "state," but instead a production process.

In Figure 3-2, quality control is shown *after* the product is produced. If this were correct, then one would inspect the product after it is completed. In reality—that is, in complex organizations with complex products—quality control is sprinkled throughout the production process, even going back as far as to Box 1. That is, a publisher does not want to solicit the "wrong," (i.e., unethical), authors, for instance—authors who could cleverly insert harmful errors in their manuscripts that would be hard to detect until the product was misused, led to injuries, or perhaps even resulted in deaths.

Boxes 12 and 13 show the transportation and distribution processes. Books, which are bulky items and in addition are shipped in large numbers, necessitate stable contracts with transportation companies, as well as with distribution or holding centers. If a publishing company is large enough, it may have regional distribution centers and, in effect, its own transportation system, if not long-term contracts with major trucking companies.

Box 13 shows that an essential part of the publishing business is advertising. In particular in the book business, this stage requires securing good reviews from critics around the country—that is, in major newspapers and magazines. This stage is anything but trivial; while one can certainly not produce favorable reviews on demand, by seeking appropriate reviews by prominent experts in universities, politics, and government, a publisher can do much to promote a book, especially by encouraging "advance buzz" or word of mouth. It is hoped that the remaining parts of the process show the generation of sales and profits, especially if a book makes it onto various bestseller lists, the most important of which is arguably the *New York Times* bestseller list. If a book is highly successful, then Box 16 indicates that the publisher may seek out and commission the same author or other authors to do other works.

The upshot of the discussion is that, whether it likes it or not, RB is potentially in a large number of businesses, many of which are related only indirectly to the book publishing industry. Also, it must be borne in mind that, as complex as Figure 3-2 is, it is still a simplified view of publishing. For one thing, the diagram makes it appear as if the process were both linear and sequential. It is not. Indeed, so many of the boxes overlap that it is not clear where one box starts and the others leave off. A more accurate representation of the process would show that all of the boxes fit within one another Thus, a better representation would be that of a hologram, where each part is contained in every other part.

Figure 3-3 makes this point even stronger. If you were to list all of the businesses that RB is in, or is contemplating entering, then you can begin to appreciate the complexity of a company like RB. As Figure 3-3 shows, publishing is indeed RB's main business—this is indicated by the box in the center of the dia-

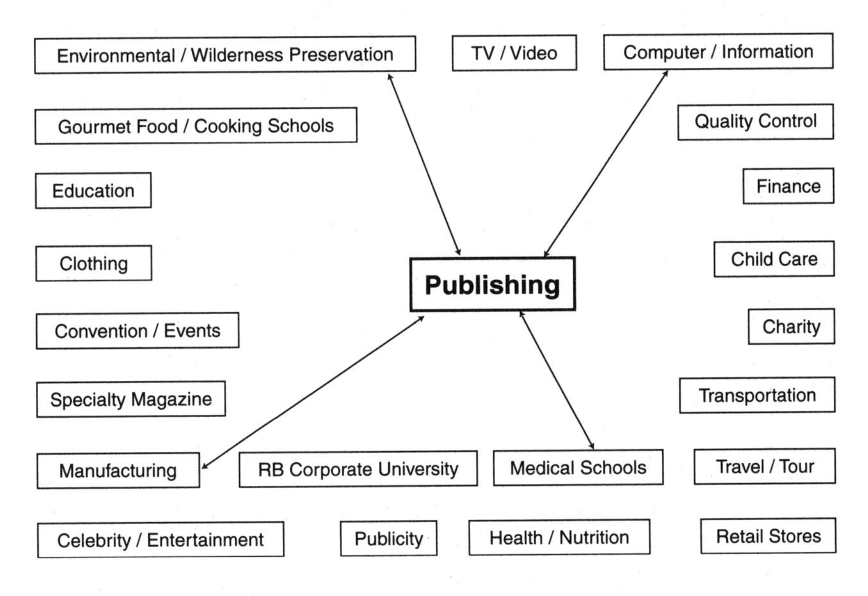

Figure 3-3. An even more realistic view of RB—the businesses RB is in.

gram. However, all of the boxes that surround the main one show the ancillary businesses that RB is involved in that facilitate the conduct of its primary business. For instance, by virtue of the kinds of books that it produces, RB is a major player in the "environmental/wilderness preservation" business. Thus, RB is a major contributor to and supporter of many environmental organizations, without which a number of them could not exist. In turn, RB depends upon their blessing and goodwill in order to conduct its business.

RB is also in the TV/video business. It has its own TV production studios. Since its books are so highly successful, it has video companions that not only show the various kinds of wild foods that are safe to eat but also how to identify them in their natural settings, and even how to prepare them.

RB is certainly in the computer/information business, and

not merely because all of its production processes are computerized. To be sure, manuscript editing is done via the computer. Computerized files are then shipped via the Internet to authors, who then review and either accept or reject the suggested editorial changes. However, in addition, RB maintains its own Web site where its products are publicized and where monthly tips are given to prospective readers so that they can keep up with the latest information on RB's products, how to cook the foods that it has identified, and so on.

RB is certainly in the quality control business. This means that quality control is an important aspect of every part of the process shown in Figure 3-2. Not only must the quality of the paper that is used in printing RB's books be extremely high so that the books will stand up under a variety of conditions, but even more important, the right information must be printed on the correct pages.

RB is also in the finance business. It has to secure capital and maintain funds on hand in order to pay advances to important authors, as well as run their main businesses, from payroll to rent to manufacturing. RB, therefore, has special arrangements with financial firms and institutions in order to manage this aspect of its business. It is also in the finance business, in that it has to raise enough capital to finance its other businesses. In addition, RB is in a number of businesses that are not as obvious from the figure. For one, RB is in the child care business. It offers child care not only for its employees but also for the crowds of people who visit RB annually.

RB decided early on to do everything possible to make it easy for prospective customers to visit its facilities, and thus, to feel part of the RB family. This parallels the actions of a company like McDonald's. Because McDonald's does a great deal of business with families with young children, it operates playgrounds—

that is, venues that give kids something to do while the rest of the family has a meal. However, few people know that McDonald's is actually the country's largest *private* playground operator. Also, because of its large number of outlets, McDonald's is one of the largest real estate *holders* in the United States and around the world. For another, McDonald's is the largest *distributor* of toys in the form of premiums. Thus, which business or businesses is McDonald's really in? The answer is, All of them!

Likewise, RB is in the charity business. Indeed, it has a major charity, and even a foundation—the RB Foundation. The charity and foundation are concerned with environmental and wilderness preservation.

RB is also in the transportation business. It not only has a considerable fleet of vans and trucks to transport its books to distribution centers, but it also provides special buses for people who want to go to local parks and national forests where the books can be used. To be sure, when RB was started, this was not something that its founders foresaw, or even wanted to do. However, as the business grew, it became obvious that RB could provide excursion buses, for which people could sign up in advance and pay a nominal fee, so they could take their purchased RBs to areas where trained guides offered tours covering the same subject matter as the books. Sales would be even greater if copies of the books were offered for sale on the buses.

This leads directly to the next box. Because of all of the buses it operates, RB is in the travel and tourism business big time. It organizes tours not only within the continental United States but also to interesting spots around the world. In this way, RB has become global. It produces RB guides for Americans and Canadians, and has branched out to books for people in over 100 countries.

RB also operates retail stores in major cities around the

country, and around the world as well. These stores not only feature RB's major products—its books—but also its caps, outerwear, and clothing. Thus, the box on the upper left side of Figure 3-3 shows that RB is now also in the clothing business because it features its own special line. RB is in the education business as well because it makes donations to schools and conducts programs at adult schools on how to prepare the foods described in its books and also how to be environmentally friendly when picking wild berries. RB is in the cooking school business, too. It has found it profitable to have cooking schools in major cities around the nation where experts at preparing wild foods can instruct readers on doing the same.

RB is in the convention/special events business. Representatives travel around the country and set up prominent displays featuring outdoor products at major conventions. Recently, RB has also entered the specialty magazine business, with a monthly magazine that features the RB site of the month, the RB cook of the month, and so on.

To be sure, RB is in the manufacturing business, which has been shown primarily in Figure 3-2. But RB is also in the celebrity/entertainment business. Like many businesses, RB has found that if it can get endorsements from or use celebrities in promoting its products, then it sells more books. However, RB is not out for the endorsement of just any celebrity. It wants celebrities who have a genuine concern for the outdoors, for maintaining the wilderness, and for saving the environment in general. This is another way RB is aiding charities that are helping preserve the environment. However, lest they be viewed as only concerned with nature, RB is also working to get inner city kids, who may never have been far from home, out into the woods to appreciate nature, often for the first time, and also gain a small modicum of relief from the dreary neighborhoods in which they live.

Although RB is primarily a publisher of field guides for wild foods, it is indirectly in the health and nutrition business. The subject matter of RB's books is not promoted as offering life's food staples; rather, wild foods are offered as a supplement to a healthy diet. But in order to accomplish this, RB has linked up with prominent nutritionists to show how these foods can be part of a healthy lifestyle.

Figure 3-3 shows only four major arrows. These arrows show how the ancillary businesses impact RB's main business. However, in reality, arrows could be drawn between *every* box in the diagram, indicating the multiple businesses that RB operates. To say that RB's business is complex is putting it mildly.

Before we leave RB's story, there is one feature of its business that is especially interesting and that particularly complicates this case study. RB not only has its own corporate college or university, where it trains workers and executives to manage its businesses, but it also has given its name to a major medical school. The school is called, appropriately enough, the RB School of Medicine. RB helped to raise the over $200 million dollars needed to construct a new building for the school. It is at Mary Douglas's alma mater. But this relationship between RB and the medical school means that if a major crisis occurs at the RB School of Medicine, it will "contaminate" or "infect" (no pun intended) RB as well. For instance, as soon as allegations were made that cadaver parts were sold illegally by persons at the UCLA School of Medicine (see the opening quotation for this chapter), local and nationwide news programs prominently featured pictures of the UCLA medical school: The David Geffen School of Medicine at UCLA. David Geffen is a powerful and wealthy member of the entertainment industry. One can well imagine how he must have felt seeing his name linked with a crisis in which he presumably had no part.

The point is that, by virtue of its strong tie with a major university, RB inherits all the opportunities, problems, and crises of a major university.

Universities as Complex Systems

Perhaps more than any other modern institution, the university illustrates how complex the world is today. Since I primarily work at a major university, I am familiar with its complexities. Figures 3-4, 3-5, and 3-6 show this complexity and all its ramifications.

Figure 3-4 shows that although education and research are the primary businesses of the modern university, the number of additional businesses that universities operate in order to accomplish their main mission is very large.

For instance, Figure 3-4 shows that most major universities are in the hotel business. They serve thousands of meals daily; they have to service hundreds of rooms, both on and off campus. Therefore, safety and security are primary concerns of most uni-

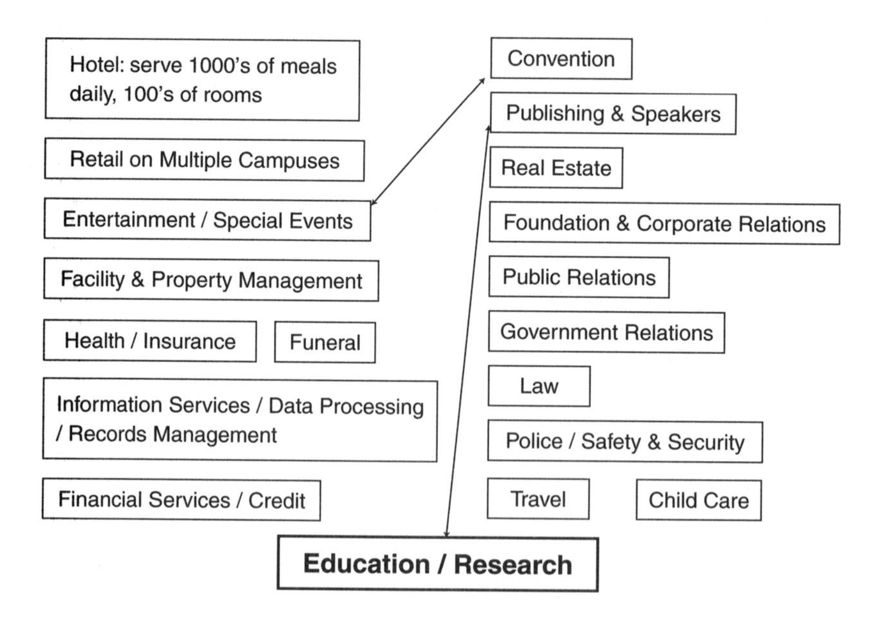

Figure 3-4. Universities as complex organizations, the large number and the wide variety of businesses.

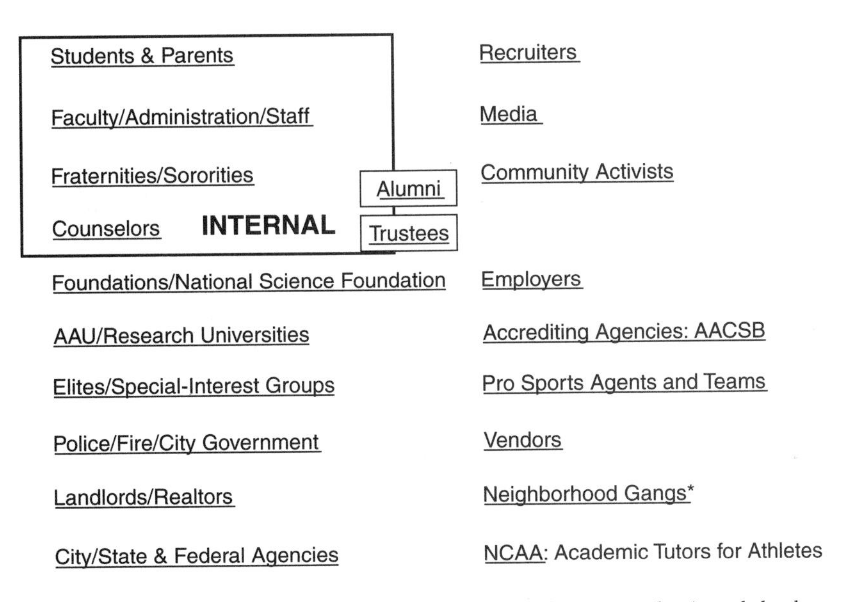

*For many urban universities, neighborhood gangs are an unfortunate and unintended stakeholder. For example, they influence the decisions of students (and their parents) whether to attend a particular university.

Figure 3-5. Universities as complex organizations, the large number and the wide variety of stakeholders.

versities. Indeed, most universities have their own police, safety, and security forces. The thousands of meals served daily are most often prepared in multiple locations. Unfortunately, this situation gives rise to the possibility of product tampering by disgruntled students or employees. Therefore, product tampering has to be taken as a real and serious possibility.

If universities are successful, whether they are prestigious academically or have a prominent sports team, or both, the subsequent retail businesses the school operates are also very important. In recent years, selling clothing with the university logo has been a huge business and includes hats, sweatshirts, license plates, and so on.

Crime: Serial rapes / murders / robberies /guns / institutional / organized / gangs / terrorism

Informational: Identity theft / tampering with confidential records / fraud / student inventories / grade tampering

Building Safety: Substandard housing / unsafe / unhealthy / on & off campus / facilities / structural integrity / backup power / failure of power generators on key buildings

Athletics: Recruiting practices / drugs / unauthorized parties

Visitors: Housing & recruiting practices / special events

Health: SARS / outbreaks / food safety & tampering

Unethical Behavior/Misconduct: Fraud by internal & external stakeholders / sexual harassment / cheating / grade inflation

Major Power Outages: Backups

Natural Disasters/Fires

Legal/Labor Disputes

Financial: Failure of a major unit / school / fraud / # of checks / transactions

Perceptual/Reputational: False rumors / stories

Figure 3-6. Potential crises—ticking time bombs for universities.

There is no question that universities are also in the entertainment and special events businesses. Sports are big business, especially if the school has nationally ranked teams. But universities also host all kinds of visitors, from important speakers to concerts, celebrity shows, traveling Broadway companies, and the like. Because most universities have large campuses, they are thereby in the facilities and property management business. Indeed, in most major cities, a university is the city's largest private employer. In fact, many major universities are on the order of billion-dollar-a-year businesses.

Universities are certainly in the health and insurance businesses because of the extensive benefits they provide to faculty, staff, students, and in some cases, trustees. If the university has a major medical school, then it is certainly in the funeral business. However, unless a crisis breaks, such as that which happened recently at UCLA, most people are totally unaware of this aspect of university business. Since bodies are often donated for medical research, they not only have to be disposed of properly but, even more important, treated with respect and dignity, in accordance with the wishes of donor families.

Figure 3-5 shows the complexities of universities from another perspective. The figure displays the tremendous variety and number of stakeholders for a modern university. Unfortunately, a crisis can happen to or be caused by any one of the stakeholders shown in Figure 3-5.

Figure 3-6 is a modest list of potential crises, or "ticking time bombs," to which universities are subject. Because of the immense complexity of businesses and the huge variety of stakeholders that a university has, the number of crises that can strike, and for which they must be prepared, is large. Indeed, Figure 3-6 shows that the possible crises span virtually all known types of crises (see Table 3-1).

Concluding Remarks

In this chapter, we have demonstrated the potential complexity of *all* businesses in today's world. This complexity has the unintended consequence that all businesses are now essentially in all other businesses, all of the time. But also, all businesses are now subject to the crises that strike all other businesses. Another way of saying this is that all crises are contained in all other crises. This is not to contend that all businesses are necessarily as complex as RB or a modern university. It is, however, to contend that most businesses are now far more complex than they wish to acknowledge.

Table 3-1. Major types of crises.

Economic	Informational	Physical	Human Resources
Labor strikes	Loss of proprietary and confidential information	Loss of key equipment, plants, and material supplies	Loss of key executives
Labor unrest	False information	Breakdowns of key equipment, plants, etc.	Loss of key personnel
Labor shortage	Tampering with computer records	Loss of key facilities	Rise in absenteeism
Major decline in stock price and fluctuations	Loss of key computer information with regard to customers, suppliers, etc.	Major plant disruptions	Rise in vandalism and accidents
Market crash	Y2K	Explosions	Workplace violence
Decline in major earnings		Faulty or poor product design	Lack of succession plans
Hostile takeovers		Product failures	Corruption
		Poor quality control	Labor strikes
			Labor unrest
			Labor shortage

Reputational	**Psychopathic Acts**	**Natural Disasters**
Slander	Product tampering	Earthquakes
Gossip	Kidnapping	Fires
Sick jokes	Hostage taking	Floods
Rumors	Terrorism	Typhoons
Damage to corporate reputation	Workplace violence	Hurricanes
Tampering with corporate logos	Criminal/ terrorist/ psychopathic acts	Mudslides
False rumors		

The world in which we now live is anything but simple. Businesses are certainly far more complex machines than as shown in Figure 3-1. Indeed, all of the figures in this chapter show that businesses today are an immensely complex system. However, this observation raises the thorny question, "How does one prepare for a seemingly *un*bounded set of crises in these complex systems?" To say that this is an important question is to put it mildly; it's a question we address in a later chapter.

This chapter has also demonstrated what risk management and security officer Bob Hunt would have had to do in order to sell a broader program of crisis management (CM) to Mary and her top executive team at RB. In effect, as best as he could have done at the time, Bob would have had to develop his own version of Figures 3-2 and 3-3. In effect, he would have had to have known as much, if not even more, about RB's businesses as Mary and her top team do. In addition, he would have had to demonstrate a plausible scenario of how each of the crises listed in Table 3-1 could happen to the full range of businesses that RB is in. In effect, he would have to sell *both* broad views of RB *and* detailed crisis scenarios. It is highly doubtful that one sale would be sufficient. As we shall see in the next chapter, this is not to say that Bob would have had to develop perfect scenarios—there is no such thing. Rather, he would have to develop scenarios over time as he learned more about the RB system and, unfortunately, as some crises developed.

In fact, if Bob Hunt were to be successful, he would have to do much more. He would have to meet on a continual basis with the other "Bob Hunts" in parallel organizations and businesses—that is, competitors as well as allies. He would have to learn from them what they had done to sell CM successfully to their respective organizations.

In short, in order to sell a broader program of CM to Mary

and her top team, Bob Hunt would have to gather information simultaneously from multiple channels regarding the desirability and necessity of such a program. In addition, executives of other organizations would have to get together on a periodic basis to share information on the crises that they have faced and why other members of the industry should consider preparing for them. Unless such information comes in from multiple channels—for instance, from industry trade associations, other executives, the news media—it is highly doubtful that an organization, even one such as RB that is in a variety of businesses and therefore has wide contacts with the world, will become fully aware of all the crises it is subject to. It will be even less likely that it will take proper action.

Bob Hunt would have to convene an internal RB stakeholder conference. He would have to interview people in all of RB's businesses in order to discover the "ticking time bombs" that they see in their respective parts of the organization. He would have to understand RB's businesses better than the various stakeholders do themselves.

To be sure, the preceding is a daunting series of tasks. But that is precisely what differentiates those organizations that are in what I call the Crisis Prepared Zone, or at the very least, are constantly striving to be in the zone, from those that are not.

Finally, one cannot help but be struck by the difference between the effectiveness with which RB conducts all of its businesses and the limited approach it takes with regard to crises. Whether it acknowledges it or not, RB is subject to a wide variety of crises precisely because of the wide variety of businesses that it is in.

Once again, we witness the denial and all the other defense mechanisms about which Freud wrote so eloquently. These mechanisms have the effect of narrowing the risks and the potential crises that RB can acknowledge. Unfortunately, defense mechanisms do not restrict crises themselves. In the end, the most critical contention that will be invalidated by RB's crisis or crises is:

You, RB, failed to make the world safe by taking an unduly narrow view of the risks to which you are subject. The limited risks that you are willing to acknowledge do not correspond to the full set of risks that you have incurred.

In this sense, RB made a false assumption: that a narrow view of risks was sufficient for the company to be protected.

Notes

1. Tom Peters and Robert Waterman, *In Search of Excellence* (New York: Warner Books, 1988).
2. John Dewey, *The Quest for Certainty* (New York: Putnam, 1999).

CHAPTER FOUR

Challenge 4

Right Integration (Integrative IQ): Embrace Fuzziness

Opening Arguments Given in AAA Wrongful-Death Suit, Tuesday, September 9, 2003—Associated Press

PLYMOUTH—A woman who was murdered in 1999 after her car broke down and she accepted help from a stranger was failed by her Auto Club, an attorney for the victim's family said during opening statements Tuesday.

The family of Melissa Gosul is suing AAA for wrongful death and negligence, claiming that if the auto association had assisted Gosul properly she would not have been raped and stabbed to death.

"This is about a nightmare that should have been prevented," said Michael Paris, the family's attorney. "All because the defendants failed to do what they were supposed to do."

But an attorney for AAA of Southern New England said Gosul, whose car broke down on Cape Cod, was in a busy recreation area on a summer evening, near a major highway, a restaurant, and a gas station.

"Melissa was not left in an unsafe location," said Robert Gainor.

On July 11, 1999, Gosul returned from a bike ride in a park to find her car would not start. Michael Gentile, who was later con-

victed for her murder, let the 27-year-old elementary school teacher use his cell phone. When the AAA tow truck driver arrived, he told Gosul he was busy and would not be able to take her or her car back to Boston for another three or four hours. Gentile eventually offered to drive Gosul home to her parents' house in Brockton.

Her body was later found in a shallow grave.

The defense said that, according to witnesses, Gosul asked others for a ride back to Boston before the tow truck operator arrived and even described Gentile to another person in the recreation area as "a guy being nice" to her.

"She was already relying on other people, other strangers, for a ride back," said Bobby R. Burchfield, attorney for the National AAA.

The lawsuit names the National AAA; its local affiliates, AAA Southern New England; and the tow truck driver. It asks for unspecified damages. The case is being watched by the legal community to see if a jury will hold AAA liable.

The great poet Rilke wrote: "Be patient towards all that is unsolved in your heart, and learn to love the questions themselves."

—Fred Rogers, *You Are Special: Words of Wisdom from America's Most Beloved Neighbor* (New York: Viking, 1994), p. 160

The Argument

1. The world is inherently fuzzy, complex, and uncertain.
2. The problems of the world are not exercises—that is, overly simplified, well-structured problems, such as those that are typically found at the end of the chapters in textbooks; for example, "$x + 6 = 11$; find x."
3. Exercises have one and only one right answer that everyone is expected to find, and hence, to agree with. (In the exercise in item 2 above, $x = 5$). This is because exercises have one and only one definition, or formulation, that is "given" to the student.
4. In contrast, problems have as at least as many definitions, or formulations, as there are major stakeholders who both affect and in turn are affected by the problem. Indeed, the more important the problem, then the more likely that each stakeholder will have a different definition. Each sees the problem from his or her unique perspective. For instance, why should we expect that every important stakeholder should have the exact same definition of what a crisis is or what a terrorist act is?
5. The problems of the world are extracted, often with extreme difficulty, from complex messes. They are "taken" from the world by humans, not "given" to us by the gods.
6. A "mess" is a complex system of problems such that no problem or part of the mess exists or can be defined independently of all the other problems that constitute

the mess! In short, messes are highly interactive systems of problems.

7. The problem with conventional education is that, for the most part, people are *trained* to solve canned exercises. They have not been educated to *formulate* complex problems. As a result, far too many people want checklists, clear-cut guides, and simple procedures for doing crisis management (CM). As a result, they want to reduce CM to a series of canned exercises.
8. Not only does the field of CM deal with problems that are inherently ill-structured and ill-defined but that CM itself is inherently ill-structured.
9. CM also deals with problems that are "messes." In fact, CM is a major form of "mess management."

William James: The Quintessential Crisis Manager

William James, the founder of that distinct brand of American philosophy known as Pragmatism, is arguably this country's greatest philosopher. (James taught at Harvard in the late 1800s and early 1900s.) He is also arguably one of the greatest philosophers that the world has ever produced. James's philosophy is extremely relevant to CM. Indeed, I would argue that James is *the* philosopher who is most relevant for CM.

James is especially known for his development of a unique theory of Truth. His is a theory of problem solving for complex problems. It is a theory of critical thinking and of how to formulate complex problems from multiple points of view. For James, a single view or perspective of any problem is automatically wrong. A single perspective cannot hope to capture all of the subtleties and the complexities that are characteristic of real problems.

Four Distinct Styles of Thinking

James began his first lecture on Pragmatism by noting two distinct types of minds, or styles of thinking, that have appeared repeatedly throughout human history: tough-minded versus tender-minded. While these two types certainly exist, and are still relevant today, modern psychologists have discovered additional dimensions that need to be added to James's system if we are to capture more completely the full range of differences that underlie human thinking. For want of better terms, I call these two additional types "earth-bound," "grounded," or "bounded" versus "airy," "floating in the clouds," or "unbounded." Thus, if we take the distinction of tough versus tender and add the two additional distinctions, bounded versus unbounded, then we get the possibility of four, not two, different types of thinkers (see Figure 4-1).

In order to understand these different ways of thinking, let us take two of them and see how they would respond to the AAA tragedy or crisis that is the opening quotation for this chapter.

- Tough-minded-earthbound types tend to frame the AAA tragedy primarily in legal terms. They are also inclined to protect the interests of AAA. As a result, they want AAA to say as little as possible so as to limit the organization's legal liabilities. In slightly different words, those who are inclined to a legal perspective often respond in a language that is perceived as cold as the

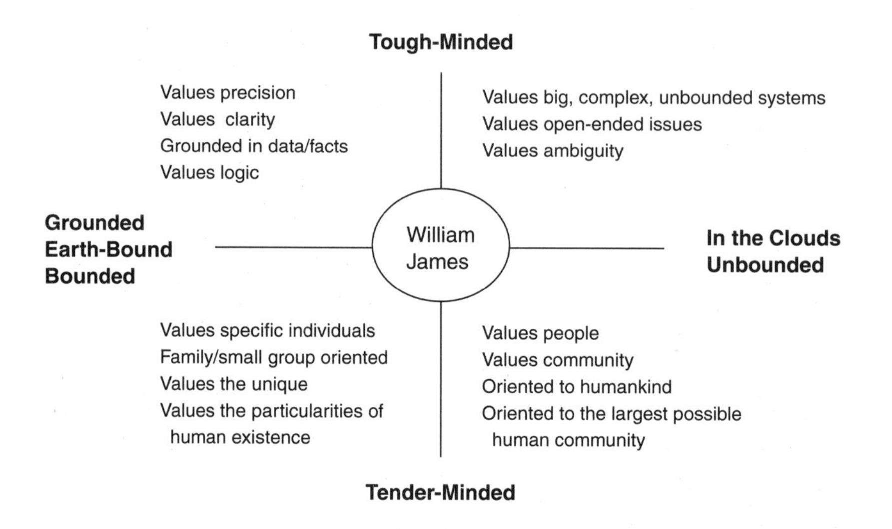

Figure 4-1. Four distinct types of thinking.

initial tragedy itself. (To be sure, lawyers representing the plaintiff's side often also use the same dry, cold language and mode of thinking to protect the injured parties. Thus, "lawyering" is not confined to protecting an organization's interests.)

■ Juxtaposed with this view is a completely opposite way of thinking, what I call the tender-minded or in-the-clouds type. This style is the complete opposite of the first. It is the contrast between the upper left-hand quadrant of Figure 4-1 and the lower right-hand.

This contrast was brought out forcefully in a recent class on critical thinking that I conducted. The students were exposed to all four of the characters or styles of thinking, as shown in Figure 4-1. They were then instructed to find a contemporary problem that they could analyze from all four perspectives. Not only were they to analyze the problem from all four perspectives, but they were to *define* the problem from each point of view. This latter task was assigned in order to ensure that the students knew how to speak each of the four "languages" represented in Figure 4-1, and by doing so, learn how to produce richer definitions of any problem.

One of the prime characteristics of complex problems is that they cannot be defined *solely* from a single perspective. Each of the four points of view naturally emphasizes certain features of a complex problem and neglects other points of view. But it is often precisely those other neglected perspectives that come back to haunt us.

One of the students in the class chose the AAA tragedy for the exercise. In the discussion that followed, an interesting approach emerged that was different from the legal perspective. To be sure, the group had gotten the legal approach down pat, because this position is not only obvious in today's world but especially so in a society as litigious as ours. In the ensuing class discussion, I raised the question, "Why didn't AAA have a van or cab service that they could offer to a stranded motorist such that, if he or she felt unsafe, the motorist could be transported to a more secure location?" (Of course, this assumes that the operators of the vans or cabs would themselves not be criminals! Chapter Five pursues this point more fully.)

At this point, one of the students in the class jumped out of her seat—and, I mean literally jumped. Not only did she stand upright but her eyes flashed as well. She blurted out, "Why didn't AAA think of using their affiliated hotels, which span the country, as potential safe havens where motorists could be taken if they desired?"

This suggestion expanded the discussion further. The whole point was that AAA already had an infrastructure that, if viewed in slightly different terms, was a natural "safe haven."[1] In other words, it takes only a slight leap of imagination to convert a system that was designed for one purpose—that is, to provide discounts to members traveling across the country for securing clean and economical lodgings, to serve another human purpose—that is, a nationwide highway safety system. However, this line of thinking raises the critical question, "Why is it that most people and most organizations aren't capable of making this leap?"

Most organizations certainly have legal counsel. This is built into their basic operating structure. The job of legal counsel is to protect the legal liabilities of an organization. On the other hand, most organizations also have public relations and human resource specialists, security departments, and so on. Why didn't any of them think about using their affiliated hotel system for another purpose? To be sure, this might have been considered impossible or even ridiculous *before* the tragedy, but it certainly cannot be considered ridiculous *after* it. If one is to learn from such tragedies in order to ensure that they will not happen again, then are not AAA and all other organizations obligated to engage in this thinking so as to mitigate future crises?

The Demise of Work and Organizations as We Have Known Them

The jobless recovery is one of the strongest signals to date that the nature of work is undergoing a major transformation—indeed, what some would call a major revolution. It is as profound and as radical a transformation as any that has occurred in human history. To say the least, it is also a crisis as profound as any that has befallen our nation. It certainly promises to alter every aspect of our lives. For another, the transformation has important ramifications for CM.

The nature of this transformation is as follows: Anything that can be defined precisely and unambiguously—that is, in tough-minded, grounded terms, can in principle be outsourced, or exported, to another country where it can be performed cheaper and, in many cases, faster than it can by U.S. workers. The truly radical nature of this transformation is that it no longer applies merely to manual or physical work, but to higher-level mental work as well. For instance, it applies to the development and manufacturing of computer software. It applies to thousands of other traditionally high-skilled jobs such as accounting, financial analysis, and engineering design. In short, anything that is well-structured and relatively independent of context and culture—that is, tough-minded, grounded thinking, can be done by someone who is not a member of the society in which the problem arose initially.

The consequences of this revolution are literally mind-boggling. For one, it threatens to demolish the stranglehold that the traditional academic disciplines have had on knowledge for hundreds of years. The organization of the modern university into separate, autonomous disciplines is as clear-cut an example of tough-minded, grounded thinking as one is ever likely to find. The boldest prediction one can make is that the modern university will cease to exist, at least in its present form.

This revolution also threatens to demolish the monopoly that the traditional disciplines have held over work. It promises to alter radically traditional corporate functions such as Accounting, Finance, Marketing, Law, and Manufacturing. In other words, it promises to change the traditional, tough-minded, grounded design that has dominated all organizations. Likewise, the changes will not be alleviated by integrating or even synthesizing diverse disciplines into new forms, such as hybrid disciplines like bioengineering (interdisciplinary).

The traditional academic disciplines, professions, and corporate functions are obsolete. If one can no longer expect to work in a single job for a single organization for one's entire life, then one can no longer expect to practice a single discipline, profession, or corporate function for one's entire life. The nature of work has changed dramatically because the nature of knowledge has changed, and vice versa.

To grasp the truly radical nature of this revolution, it is necessary to understand that multi- and interdisciplinary approaches to knowledge will not solve the fundamental problem we are facing. That fundamental problem will not be alleviated be combining or bringing more disciplines to bear on an issue (multidisciplinary approach). Likewise, it will not be solved by integrating or synthesizing diverse disciplines into new forms (interdisciplinary). Instead, our problems will begin to be solved only when we finally realize, and accept, that virtually all problems lie beyond the reach of *any* currently known disciplines, professions, and functions. Furthermore, the problems will be solved only when we realize that solutions lie beyond any disciplines, professions, or functions that we can even *begin* to imagine. As a result, we need to develop both the concepts and the understanding of what it is to know something without disciplines, professions, and traditional job descriptions.[2]

The only reliable predictions regarding the types of jobs that will remain in the United States are those that satisfy two conditions:(1) those that require an in-depth, working knowledge of U.S. culture; and (2), those that require high-level, critical thinking and creative judgment. In short, we need to learn desperately how to apply all four types of thinking (see Figure 4-1) to all problems. Anything else is doomed to vanish—forever!

Diminished Expectations, Vanishing Dreams

By now, the stories are all too familiar: the permanent loss of hundreds of thousands of high-paying white-collar jobs to Asian and Third World countries; the greatly increased time that it takes to land a similar job at an equivalent rate of pay, if such jobs even exist. Today we face the substantial lowering of expectations, the fact that often the only jobs available are those considerably below one's level of education, job experience, and previous income; consequently, there's the fact that millions of people have completely given up all hope of finding a job and have therefore dropped out of the labor force.

The moral of the preceding is not that individual job seekers are bad or are failures. It is that the nineteenth- and twentieth-century notions of knowledge and education are not adequate to solve the problems and provide the jobs for the twenty-first century. It is the system, not individuals, that has failed. This chapter is necessarily philosophical, for the root of our problems is our outmoded assumptions or, more precisely, our undue reliance on outmoded assumptions.

Outmoded Assumptions

The thinking of the nineteenth and twentieth centuries developed a view of problems that influenced profoundly the nature of education and work. This view is best stated in terms of the key assumptions upon which it was based:

1. In order for something to be or to count as a problem, it had to be stated (defined) unambiguously and precisely; unless one could state or define a problem in this manner, one could not know what the problem was, and hence, would not know what the solution was, if one existed; in other words, problems had to be stated in tough-minded, grounded terms.

2. The best (superior) language for stating problems was mathematics; the ideal model was Euclid's geometry, where one started proofs with intuitively obvious or self-evident ideas (axioms and postulates), such as the definitions of points, lines, or triangles, and from these one derived rigorously (deductively) a potentially infinite set of interesting and important conclusions known as theorems. In the more extreme versions of this philosophy of problems, unless something could be expressed in the rigorous and exacting language of mathematics, it was not worthy of the term "problem."

3. All complex problems were in principle decomposable into a finite set of separate and simpler problems. The "sum" (synthesis) of the solutions to the separate and simpler problems was then the solution to the complex problem. In fact, for something even to be considered as a problem, it *had to be* decomposable into its simpler problems or "atoms."

4. Different disciplines owned different atoms; different disciplines owned different types of problems. As a corollary, the different disciplines were clearly separable from one another. Finally, there was a strict hierarchy between disciplines; some disciplines were better than others. "Better" meant that one discipline could state its problems more rigorously (e.g., in terms of mathematics) than others; conversely, the more a discipline could state its problems independently of context, the better it was as well.

5. Education consisted largely of solving a set of pre-defined exercises (e.g., "$x + 6 = 11$; find x"). By definition, exercises have one formulation (the one that is *given* to students in textbooks), and as a result, exercises have only one right answer.

6. A problem once solved remained solved forever in the same way that a set of facts once established presumably was established forever; for instance, the boiling point of water is a constant, not a variable.

Counterassumptions

This book is based on a complete set of counterassumptions:

1. A fundamental characteristic of problems is that when they first arise, they are highly ambiguous; in other words, problems are not separable from ambiguity. Indeed, if anything, problems are extracted from ambiguity. For something to be a problem it has to be infused with ambiguity, for the nature of most complex problems is not clear or well known in the beginning. This certainly applies to crises; rarely is the full nature of a crisis known when it first presents itself.

2. There is no one best or superior language in which to state a problem. The notion of a "best language" already assumes that one knows that the problem is or, at the very least, knows a great deal about it. Certainly, most of our critical problems cannot be stated unambiguously, let alone in the restricted language of mathematics.

3. In principle, complex problems are not decomposable into a finite set of separate and simpler problems. To the contrary, by definition, complex problems must be treated as "wholes"—in other words, complex problems possess properties as a whole that none of the parts do.

4. Different disciplines do not necessarily "own" different parts of complex problems because the disciplines themselves are largely artifacts. If complex problems exist only as "wholes," then the knowledge required for formulating and solving problems must be holistic as well. The different disciplines are not clearly separable from one another; there is no strict hierarchy between disciplines such that some are better than others. Mathematical rigor is not necessarily the most desirable skill in formulating or in solving problems.

5. Education first and foremost consists of critical thinking. A critical part of critical thinking is problem formulation—that is, one learns how to formulate problems from at least each of the four different styles of thinking. By definition, complex problems do not have a single formulation.

6. Problems do not remain solved. Indeed, in the process of working on a problem, one discovers that the nature of the problem, let alone the solution, changes substantially.

The Management of Truth

The moral of the story so far is that for William James, epistemology—or that branch of philosophy that deals with the nature of truth, what it is, and how we humans can obtain it—is actually the *management of truth!*

If ever a concept had a dangerous and an ominous ring, then surely it is the "management of truth." It implies that humans manipulate the truth solely for evil ends. While to be sure this often happens, the inescapable fact is that truth is a thoroughly human creation. Whether humans manipulate the truth or not, that humans make Truth is uncontestable. They create it through their actions in an attempt to achieve desired ends. For James,

Truth is not an abstract concept that is independent of human purposes and ends. Truth is not something that is "just out there."

Truth is in fact the management of ways and styles of knowing. Knowledge cannot be decoupled from knowers—that is, from the processes by which humans know things. Truth is thus the management of at least four different types of knowers.

This is precisely what makes James so powerful and his ideas so relevant to CM.

The Crucial Differences Between Well-Structured and Ill-Structured Problems

Real problems are by their very nature ill-structured or ill-defined. At least in the very beginning, when problems first present themselves, they are not already or automatically well-defined or well-structured. (When we say a problem is well-structured, we mean it is expressed in an exact language—for instance, algebra or mathematics, such that it yields an exact solution. An example is that of the field of corporate finance, in which one computes the present value of a future amount of money, knowing today's interest rate and how far into the future one is discounting back into the present.)

Consider a person who is pondering the choice between available means, or courses of action, to get downtown in the shortest time possible. Figures 4-2 and 4-3 are two different ways of representing the same problem (Figure 4-2 is called a tree representation while Figure 4-3 is a matrix). The person has three available means to get downtown: (1) drive his or her car; (2) walk; or (3) take a bus. Suppose, in addition, that there are three mutually exclusive outcomes: (1) get downtown in twenty minutes or less; (2) get downtown in exactly twenty minutes;

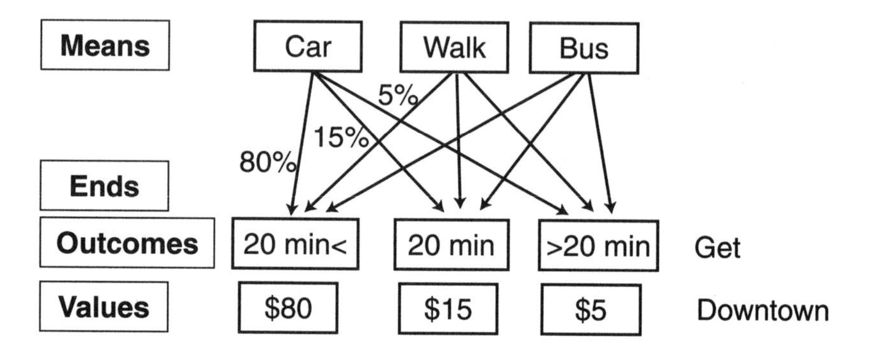

Figure 4-2. A well-structured problem—tree representation.

		Ends			
	Values	$80	$15	$5	= $100
	Outcomes	20 <	20 min	> 20	
Means	P(Car) = 0.8	80%	15%	5%	Sum % = 100%
	P(Walk) = 0.1	0%	1%	99%	Sum % = 100%
	P(Bus) = 0.1	40%	40%	20%	Sum % = 100%
	Sum P = 1.0				

Figure 4-3. A well-structured problem—matrix representation.

and (3) get downtown in more than twenty minutes. Suppose also that the person places the value of getting downtown in less than twenty minutes at $80; exactly twenty minutes at $15; and finally getting downtown in greater than twenty minutes at $5. Suppose also, as shown in Figure 4-3, that if one takes a car, then there is an 80 percent chance of getting downtown in less than twenty minutes, a zero percent chance if one walks, and a 40 percent chance if one takes a bus.

The point is that only for well-structured problems—that is, exercises—do we know all of the available courses of action, their outcomes, their consequences, and their benefits versus costs associated with them. In contrast, an ill-structured problem is precisely a problem for which the full set of means is not known, or only partially known. In addition, the ends are not fully known, let alone their consequences. Thus, Figures 4-2 and 4-3 do not represent real-world problems.

All of Us Are Problem Managers

All of us are not merely problem solvers, which we are, but rather are also problem managers. Even more basic, we are "problem creators" and "problem organizers." Whatever structure or definition a problem possesses is due to our efforts. Problems become defined and structured through our efforts—that is, through the process of our working on them.

The problems of the world are not normally the captive of a single academic discipline—for example, psychology—or a single corporate function, such as Finance. No single discipline "owns" the problem of world hunger, for instance. The problem of world hunger cannot be defined completely or adequately by any single discipline. Most real-world issues are complex mixtures of different disciplines and functions—they are interdisciplinary and cross functional. Even more to the point, they are transdisciplinary. That is, they are beyond any of the known disciplines.

The same is also true of CM—that is, CM is inherently transdisciplinary. This means that CM cannot be represented in the form of either Figures 4-2 or 4-3. For another, it means that different stakeholders will have different versions of Figures 4-2 and 4-3, if they exist at all. Different stakeholders do not see the same courses of action or the same outcomes of the "same" crisis.

For instance, RB's crisis is not a single problem or a single crisis. Instead, it is a whole system of problems and crises that are highly interdependent and interactive. One cannot even begin to define RB's crisis, let alone pretend to manage it, independently of all the other problems and crises to which it is connected and to which it gives rise.

The Basic Problem of Ill-Structured Problems

The basic problem with ill-structured problems the presence of strong conflict over the definition as to the nature of the problem. The steps of (1) problem formulation and (2) problem representation are thus central facing ill-structured problems.

In contrast to well-structured problems, different stakeholders generally define ill-structured problems differently—often radically differently—depending upon their values, interests, education, personal history, and the organization for which they work, to mention only a few of the many relevant factors. For this and many other reasons, ill-structured problems are inherently controversial. As a result, we would not expect two stakeholders to define an ill-structured problem in exactly the same way. In fact, we would suspect collusion if they did.

For the same reason, we would not expect two or more CM scholars, experts, or practitioners to have the same definition of what is a crisis, a disaster, or a minor problem. The repeated calls for agreement with regard to basic definitions of what is a crisis ignore the basic character of ill-structured problems. Ill-structured problems are problems for which fundamental differences not only exist but predominate. Indeed, intense disagreement is one of the major features of ill-structured problems.

To insist therefore on agreement as a precondition for studying an ill-structured problem is to ignore and deny its basic nature. It misrepresents the problem ontologically—that is, its reality. If we could obtain prior agreement on the nature of a problem, then it would not be ill-structured. By definition, well-structured problems are problems for which we can obtain widespread agreement.

When CM scholars, experts, and practitioners call for agreement on the definition of basic terms, in effect they are committing the same errors as academics who accuse practitioners of ignoring the complexity of a crisis. We have to learn to study and then manage ill-structured problems on their own grounds.

So, disagreement regarding the nature of a problem is one of the fundamental characteristics of an ill-structured problem. Furthermore, these disagreements will not go away as the result of "better" or "more extensive" or more "precise" analyses. "Better" analyses will only reveal further and deeper disagreements.

Problems are Messes

Crises possess another essential characteristic that makes them difficult, but not necessarily impossible, to study. Crises are not only ill-structured problems but messes as well. At the very least, they are parts of messes.

The eminent systems scientist Russ Ackoff defines a mess as a system of problems that is highly interactive—that is, strongly coupled. In other words, a mess is the *product* of the interactions among all of the various problems that constitute the mess. In short, *a crisis is an ill-structured mess*, a highly interactive set of problems each of which is ill-structured in itself.

The systems philosopher C. West Churchman has put the matter even more forcefully: "Something is a problem if and only if it is a member of the set of all other problems." Thus, something is not a problem, but instead an academic exercise, if it can be defined precisely and independently of at least one other complex problem.

Concluding Remarks

This chapter has argued that our understanding of CM as a complex process and system has suffered seriously owing to the presumption of an outmoded and false philosophy regarding the nature of problems. Indeed, the field of CM will continue to stagnate if we do not revise our underlying assumptions.

Crisis management is essentially a theory of complex problems (see Appendix C). Even more basic, it is a theory of critical thinking. This appreciation is absolutely essential to the management of fuzziness, for fuzziness is an inherent property of real-world problems.

The conclusion here is that there are no exact checklists for CM (see Figure 4-4). That is, CM cannot be confined to the upper left-hand quadrant of Figure 4-4. In the truest sense of the term, CM is open-ended, unbounded problem formulation (see the right-hand quadrants of Figure 4-4). In fact, RB was already practicing a version of the thinking mode in the right-hand quadrants of Figure 4-1 when it took an uncharacteristically broad view of the expansion of its business. In contrast, it took an exceedingly narrow view of the risks—that is, the thinking mode in primarily the upper left-hand quadrant of Figure 4-4—when it came to considering the potential crises that the company could experience. In addition, it compounded the problem by making the fatal mistake of limiting to natural disasters the crises and risks it could face.

Everything connected with CM is inherently fuzzy. For instance, what is a crisis? What is the definition of a crisis? What is an early warning signal that a particular crisis is about to happen? These serious issues are fundamentally matters of judgment. This does not mean that there are no guidelines in responding to critical issues. Instead, such guidelines can only be based on heuristics, or rules of thumb. In other words, CM cannot be reduced to the approach in the upper left-hand quadrant of Figures 4-1

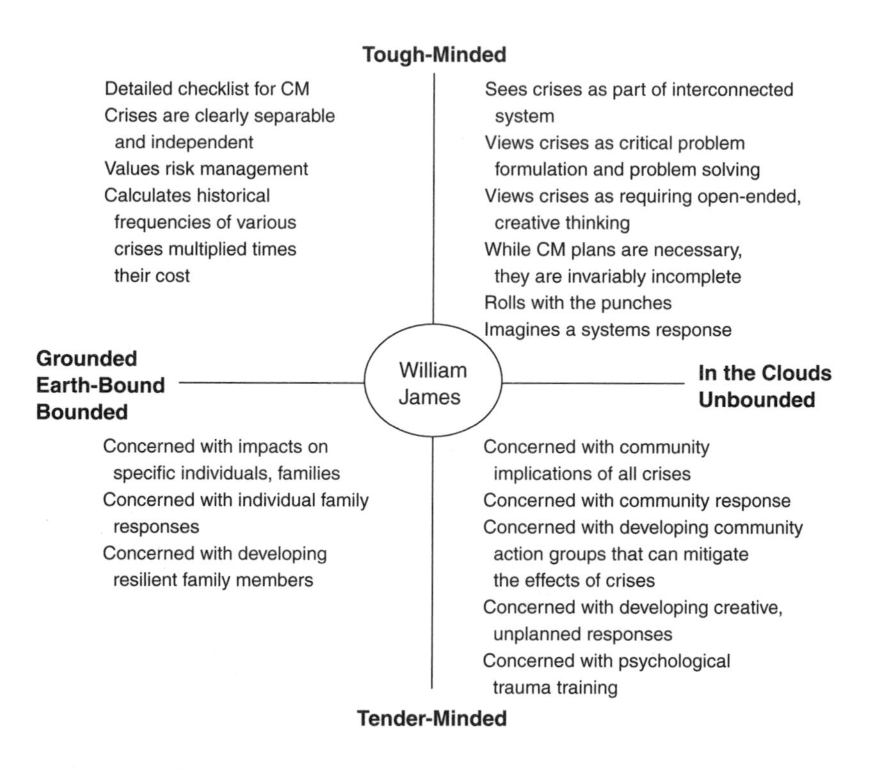

Figure 4-4. Four distinct types of thinking.

and 4-4. Unfortunately, this is what the majority of the existing books on CM would have us believe.

To put it mildly, crises are slippery. This is, in fact, one of their prime properties. And as I have emphasized, every crisis is in effect a part of every other crisis! If every business is now in every other business, then every business has the potential to experience the crises of every kind of business! This is precisely why the kind of thinking presented in the right-hand sides of Figures 4-1 and 4-4 is so important. Crises demand that we take an expansive view of the world.

This chapter has also demonstrated the severe split that we discussed in Chapter Two. Namely, that there is a contradiction in RB's mental outlook: the kind of thinking that it uses to conduct its business versus the outlook that it has used to think about and to prepare for crises. Whereas it uses the right-hand side of Figure 4-1 to think broadly about its businesses, it uses the upper left-hand quadrant of Figure 4-1 when thinking about crises. This is because RB has not yet confronted, let alone mastered, its underlying emotions, fears, and anxieties with regard to crises.

This split is characteristic of the vast majority of businesses. It is the divergence between creativity and thinking about risks. Whereas most businesses are willing to court risks when it comes to conducting everyday business, they are extremely risk adverse when it comes to thinking about crises. Whereas they are unconventional in their thinking about business, they are conventional when it comes to thinking about crises.

In the end, RB will have one of its major assumptions invalidated by its crisis:

You, RB, failed to make the world safe by adopting a predominantly upper left-hand quadrant approach to crises. In short, you were too myopic in your thinking.

Notes

1. Walter Kirn, "Birth of a Vacation: Holiday Inn Made It Safe for Americans to Go on the Road," *New York Times Magazine*, December 28, 2003, p. 12.

2. See Ian I. Mitroff and Harold Linstone, *The Unbounded Mind: Breaking the Chains of Traditional Business Thinking* (New York: Oxford University Press, 1995).

CHAPTER FIVE

Challenge 5

Right Technical Skills (Technical IQ): Think Like a Sociopath, Act Like a Saint

A degree of paranoia helps protect organizations.

—Yiannis Gabriel, *Organizations in Depth: the Psychoanalysis of Organizations* (London: Sage Publications, 1999), p. 209

Because fear is terrorism's only weapon, the terrorist's primary job (as with an infectious agent) is merely to initiate the contagion. The contaminated body's immune system does the rest as the body struggles to neutralize the infection by making war on its own infected systems.

—Benjamin R. Barber, *Fear's Empire: War, Terrorism, and Democracy* (New York, W.W. Norton, 2003), p. 24

"A person using the sub-vocal system thinks of phrases and talks to himself so quietly he cannot be heard, but the tongue and vocal chords do receive speech signals from the brain," said developer Chuck Jorgensen, of NASA's Aames Research Center, Moffat Field, California.

Jorgensen's team found that sensors under the chin and on each side of the Adam's Apple pick up the brain's command to the speech organs, allowing the sub-auditory or "silent speech" to be captured.

Yahoo! News, March 17, 2004

The Argument

1. Chapters Two and Three demonstrated that one of the most significant barriers to effective crisis management (CM) is denial.
2. In order to break through denial, one first needs to find ways of intensifying potential crises without becoming paralyzed. To magnify crises without being overwhelmed by them is precisely why one needs the psychological pre-crisis training described in Chapter Two.
3. More generally, to confront the abnormal demands that we learn to think like sociopaths and terrorists without actually becoming them. In short, the task is to think like a *controlled paranoid*. The benefit of this type of thinking is that it helps one to identify a much broader range of threats against one's person, against the organization, institutions, and various societies of which one is a member.
4. This way of thinking is available *only* to individuals, organizations, institutions, and societies that are "healthy" (see Chapter Two) and "ethical." Unhealthy and unethical persons cannot hope to think like a controlled paranoid and escape unharmed. Unethical and unhealthy individuals will only become sicker and more unethical in the process. They will self-destruct.

The tenets of crisis management that have been developed for treating normal accidents are no longer sufficient. What is needed is the ability to think comprehensively about normal *and* abnormal accidents. Most companies develop and refine plans to improve the ways in which they handle emergencies of the kind they have confronted in the past. But they now face bigger threats from calamities they have never faced before or, worse, from crises they cannot even begin to imagine that they might have to cope with. As a result, they are, essentially, fighting new wars with old strategies.

Creative Demolition: A Crisis Tool Kit

Companies—all organizations in general—need to develop special skills to come to grips with abnormal accidents. In the rest of this chapter, we describe how some businesses have learned to think about the unthinkable by forcing executives to change their frames of reference. As these companies demonstrate, the key lays not so much in drafting manuals as in developing learning processes that give executives the mental capabilities, confidence, and flexibility to envisage abnormal crises.

Wheel of Crises

Some companies prepare effectively for abnormal crises by thinking about them at random. That helps because most executives are so conditioned to do conventional crisis planning that they do not know how to start imagining unfamiliar dangers without seeming to be paranoid, or they can analyze them only in limited ways. A carefully orchestrated use of the random-selection technique can help shift their reference point and force them out of their mental straitjackets.

One tool my colleagues and I have used to help top-level executives think randomly is a giant wheel of crises. We literally build a wheel, like the spinner on a child's game, and list on it all the families of crises that a company can face (see Table 3-1). Executives take turns spinning the wheel; when the pin stops, participants discuss all of the normal and abnormal crises of that particular kind that they can imagine. No possibility, however bizarre, is excluded because each thought helps overturn the executives' fundamental belief that they already know—that is, they are certain—what the crises are that the company could face.

In the next stage of this version of the exercise, the participants force together two or more abnormal crises to create an increasingly improbable combination. This both raises the magnitude of the peril and compels executives to accept that abnormal disasters often happen on a large scale. It also helps them to link crises that they never envisioned could apply to their company or to their industry. Chillingly, executives at one *Fortune* 500 company that we worked with before 9/11 combined a car bomb and an aircraft hijacking to come up with the threat of a "flying bomb" that was distressingly close to the World Trade Center attack. Unfortunately, although the crisis was discussed in some detail, it was rejected as too improbable.

The random-selection model can also be the basis of a rational budgeting strategy for an illogical world. Each year, smart companies focus their safety-control resources on a few facilities picked at random, just as airlines carry out detailed security checks on a few passengers for each flight. That reduces the probability of an attack on the entire organization as it allows the business to migrate gradually to a higher level of crisis readiness. After one global corporation evaluated the vulnerability of its 100-plus facilities to terrorist strikes, for instance, it realized that it could not afford to immediately upgrade the security and crisis response levels at all of them. However, the company did not allocate its annual CM budget of $5 million in proportion to the weaknesses of each site. Instead, it announced that half would be spent on sites the company had randomly selected and the other half on the most vulnerable ones. In the process, the company created a stronger deterrent without increasing its budget.

Internal Assassins

Many of the crisis-prepared companies that my colleagues and I have worked with rely on their people, who know the organization best, to develop abnormal situations that they should prepare for. However, employees need to be trained to imagine the worst (see Chapter Two), since they usually apply their knowledge of the company for its benefit, not its destruction. Special techniques like role-playing can get them to think (temporarily) like villains.

We often ask small groups of top or middle-level executives to imagine themselves as internal assassins or terrorists. That frees them to suspend their rational thinking and moral codes, and it allows them to use their intimate knowledge of the company's products, procedures, and systems to cook up ways to destroy it, either from the inside or the outside. In one large U.S. company, for example, we designated a group of ten senior executives as internal assassins. We walked the group through several of the company's manufacturing facilities, both during the workday and after hours. As the executives began to see the plants through terrorist's eyes, they almost reluctantly started pointing out where they would cause the most damage, how they could do so, and the entry and escape routes they would use. The scenarios were frightening, both because they exposed weaknesses in the system and because they were plausible.

The "internal assassin" technique can often change the organization's attitude toward crises. Take the case of a $1 billion U.S. medical insurance company, which used the exercise to work out if financial fraud could force it into bankruptcy as Barings, the British merchant bank, was in 1995. The company set up three teams, each consisting of eight senior executives. Team A was to devise swindles that crooked employees could carry out; Team B was to devise schemes that crooked outsiders could mount; and Team C was to develop schemes that crooked outsiders and insiders could do in collusion. Much to everyone's surprise and embarrassment, all of the teams quickly came up with ingenious scams that the organization was not currently able to detect.

The insurance company immediately formed three counter-assassin teams to develop systems to prevent or detect the swindles. After several months, these groups independently concluded that the company was most vulnerable to one fundamental situation. If a scamster was patient, he or she could accumulate a considerable fortune by siphoning off small amounts of money over long periods of time, no matter what particular scheme was used. Consequently, the company lowered detection thresholds across the organization. Managers modified computer systems to flag suspicious transactions, however small they might be, and instituted auditing procedures to examine small payouts as closely as large ones. By looking at its vulnerabilities systematically, the bank was able to close the door on an entire category of threats.

Mixed Metaphors

Most crisis-prepared companies regularly send executives to crisis forums, where companies from diverse industries discuss crisis planning. But they don't stop at that. They also rigorously apply the metaphors and lexicons of other industries to examine themselves from unusual perspectives, and they learn from the scenarios that other companies have prepared for. For instance, banks may be equipped to handle cyberattacks because computer crime is easy to imagine in the context of the financial services industry. But they may be less likely to think about explosions, which would spring immediately to the minds of executives at, say, chemical companies.

When companies look at crises that occur outside of their own industry, then some of them begin to realize how vulnerable they truly are. (This is indeed one of the main points of Chapter Three.) Take the case of a large U.S. electronics manufacturer that chose to envision itself in the food industry. (Note that this is an interesting case of the reversal of RB's situation.) If it were making food products, the company felt, its quality assurance objective would no longer be the reduction of hardware defects. It would be the elimination of latent bugs and microbes that were festering inside products and polluting them. That difference so intrigued executives that they hired an infectious disease specialist to assess how the company could prevent pathogens from contaminating their production systems and infecting their products. During the rather unusual scrutiny, the company learned that pathogens could be deliberately injected into their products, turning them into Trojan horses that transmitted disease rather than well-being—a possibility that food and drug companies routinely envision, but not manufacturers of electronics.

The alarmed giant decided to come up with ways to prevent such crises. One "pathogen" it identified was the possibility that a disgruntled employee or supplier would deliberately introduce faulty components into a product. As an "inoculation" against this event, the company stipulated that executives must determine if product failures had been deliberately caused, once customers reported a certain number of them. In addition, products that had not been shipped would be "quarantined" until the inoculation had been administered. Applying the food industry's metaphors helped the electronics giant come to terms with the threat of product tampering.

Spy Games

Proactive companies aren't shy about bringing in outsiders to test their vulnerability to abnormal crises. They realize that sometimes employees possess too much knowledge about the organization or are too steeped in everyday operations to adopt radically different perspectives. The creative use of impartial experts helps companies overcome both the "That doesn't happen here!" and the "That can't happen!" syndromes—that is, denial.

Smart companies hire professionals such as investigative journalists, lawyers, and consumer affairs experts to stage hypothetical attacks on them. Such simulations expose weaknesses and test responses at the same time. Some companies commission journalists to write investigative stories or produce 20-second videos that attack products, top executives, or reputations. The writers base their articles on actual attacks by disgruntled employees or business rivals. The intense drama of the exercises helps executives break through their disbelief and accept that they might well have to tackle such crises someday.

Other organizations ask journalists to report on their crisis prevention plans or their level of security consciousness. That helps companies almost as much as internal CM audits do. Here's what one reporter hired to snoop around one of a U.S. company's major facilities found: "A large number of files containing confidential information, sometimes dating back a decade or more, have been dumped in a basement in the main building. But there are few security checks in place. Any employee—and almost any visitor—could get at them if he or she wanted to. In fact, I was offered a random assortment of files for a small sum of money." No one in the company had realized how vulnerable those files were. Two months later, a disgruntled employee was caught trying to access some of the documents.

The criminal mind-set is so different from most people's that executives can often figure it out only by bringing it inside the organization. Banks hire former robbers to test security procedures. Casinos in Las Vegas use professional gamblers to fight cardsharpers. Insurance companies recruit reformed scamsters to detect fraud. Many companies have used professional hackers to probe the safety of their computer networks. The results are startling. For instance, when ace-hackers-turned-security-consultants have identified the areas in a company that are most susceptible to hacking, it hasn't been the software or the systems. It has been unwitting employees—hardly what most information technology managers think is a threat to computer networks.

Thinking Like a Controlled Paranoid

Paranoids suffer from a tragic and debilitating disease.[1] It exercises a nearly complete, disastrous hold on their thinking. Someone who is truly paranoid—that is, an actual paranoid—is unable to make use of the *concept* of paranoia as a tool for uncovering the weaknesses and vulnerabilities of persons, organizations, institutions, and even whole societies. In contrast to controlled paranoids, actual paranoids are not able to help us acknowledge and prepare for real threats in today's world.

But there is a framework for thinking like a paranoid without actually being or becoming one. This framework is based upon the known types of paranoia.[2] Unfortunately, the framework has not been applied systematically to businesses so that they can identify and prepare for a broad range of threats.

The Different Types of Paranoia

There are four basic types of paranoia. In addition, each type has three degrees of intensity. Thus, there are twelve kinds of paranoia.

The *first* type of paranoia pertains to a person's body. Under the lowest level, or intensity, the person feels that others are "reading or monitoring" his bodily states or functions—for example, his brainwaves, heartbeats, and so on. Under the second level, the person feels that others are attempting to "take control of or even infiltrate" his bodily functions, states, processes, and so on. Under the highest level, the person feels that others are attempting to "alter radically, redesign, or even destroy" his body.

Many organizations that operate in unsafe, typically hostile, foreign environments (e.g., Colombia) in effect use the first type to imagine all kinds of physical threats to their employees—kidnappings, murders, and the like. Without actually being paranoid themselves, they imagine the worst that can happen to their employees' "physical bodies," and they take appropriate protective measures to lower the odds of anything actually happening. They do this via several means—for example, picking up their employees at random hours, driving to and from work in special bulletproof-reinforced cars, and varying the day-to-day routes that are used to transport employees.

The *second* type of paranoia pertains to a person's immediate family, extended family, the organization(s) in which he or she works, all of the institutions with which he or she makes daily contact, and so on. That is, the second type pertains to organizations and institutions external to one's immediate body and person.

As before, all three levels of intensity apply. For example, under the first level, various scenarios are constructed as to how an unauthorized person or persons could gain access to an organization by, say, penetrating the security fences around a company. For the most part, most organizations do a fairly good job of responding to this type of threat.

The *third* type of paranoia pertains to the culture of an organization, institution, and even society itself. In this type, others attempt to "pollute the 'mind' of a culture, undermine its beliefs, way of life," and so on. An unfortunate example is the abuse of Iraqi prisoners by American troops. In fact, this is an example of "self-pollution"—that is, when a culture undermines its own claimed beliefs of respecting other cultures and their ways of life.

The *fourth* type of paranoia pertains to the mind of a single individual. For instance, under the first level of intensity, others read or monitor his thoughts. Under the second level, others attempt to take control of his thoughts. And finally, under the last level of intensity, others attempt to change his brain structure itself by, for example, implanting electronic chips that radically alter the structure of his mind.

It is precisely types 3 and 4 that organizations have the most difficulty in imagining because they pertain to the "minds" of unsavory individuals such as psychopaths and terrorists. In effect, types 3 and 4 represent the blind sides of organizations. Thus, consideration of these types is precisely the help that organizations most need.

All of these types of paranoia apply equally to individuals, organizations, institutions, and even whole societies. As farfetched as the preceding may seem, unfortunately they are no longer the province of paranoids alone. For example, we are deep into the age of bio design.[3] It is no longer the stuff of science fiction that bugs implanted in food products could be ingested such that the body becomes a biocontaminant.[4] Likewise, it is no science fiction to think about mind or body control. We are just a stone's throw from when chips can be implanted in a person's body presumably to monitor one's health.[5] And it takes just a small leap of imagination to see these devices used for unauthorized purposes.

While not a guarantee, for there are none in CM, thinking like a controlled paranoid opens up a richer, if not a more bizarre, set of potential crises. For example, NASA is on the verge of developing technology that can read subvocal words before they are actually mouthed (see the opening quotations to this chapter). Thus, the first type of paranoia—actually reading or monitoring one's brainwaves—is no longer the stuff of science fiction. We are on the verge of making it into a reality.

I cannot overemphasize that thinking like a controlled paranoid is merely one, but one of the most powerful, ways of managing fear. On the one hand, too little fear leads to denial. On the other hand, too much leads to paralysis. Thus, one of the prime purposes of emotional or psychological preparation for crises (see Chapter Two) is the ability to confront fear directly without being overwhelmed by it.

In today's world, there is no longer any question that we have to consider the unpalatable possibility that the bodies of people cannot only transport bombs but literally be bombs. Therefore, we have no choice but to view people as unpalatable delivery and arming systems themselves—in the broadest possible sense, we have to view people as walking, brewing bombs. In other words, controlled paranoids are not only paranoid about what threats exist but also with regard to how those threats are delivered. In this sense, they are paranoid about everything.

Here's one of the principal ways of thinking like a controlled paranoid: *Take every proposed action, or agent, that you can use to protect yourself from a major threat, and then flip its properties on its head*! For instance, Cipro is an effective agent in treating anthrax.[6] However, thinking like a controlled paranoid leads one to ask, "What if Cipro itself were tampered with such that what was supposed to be an antidote became another threat?"

Unfortunately, there are only a few organizations that have incorporated thinking like a controlled paranoid into their day-to-day operations. One, for instance, is a prominent theme park. It now identifies every unaccompanied male entering the park as someone to be closely monitored. This is a direct precaution against both abduction of children and pedophilia.

For another, some theme parks have security guards dressed as tourists mingle with crowds. Indeed, some parks even use a group of what appear to be tourists from another country as a team of disguised security experts. Upon a moment's notice, the group of "foreign visitors" can move to any part of the park that is under threat. In this way, the park cleverly disguises its method of counterattack. In other words, the protection of the park, while certainly far from perfect, is built into its everyday operations. In effect, this is a rather dramatic reversal of the recommendations of Charles Perrow.

Recall from Chapter One that Perrow pointed out how, in normal accidents, the potential for major crises is literally built into the day-to-day operations of organizations because of their complex technologies. In contrast, the theme park in the preceding example has built its protection into its everyday operations.

Thinking like a controlled paranoid leads one to raise all kinds of enticing questions. For instance, How can someone gain entry into the most seemingly secure systems with as little chance as possible of being stopped? The answer that one ingenious organization came up with is, Dress like a Domino Pizza delivery person! Apparently, Domino Pizza delivery people are regularly ushered into the most secure environments without being stopped.

Thinking the Absurd

In 1971, an obscure professor of philosophy, Murray S. Davis, published an article in an equally obscure academic journal with the tantalizing title, "That's Interesting!" The subtitle of the article bore the awkward phrase, "Towards a Phenomenology of Sociology and a Sociology of Phenomenology."[7] Davis put forth a stunning, if not controversial, thesis. He asserted that, strictly speaking, none of the theories in science were "true." This was especially the case in the social sciences.

No matter how good they appear to be, all theories in science are only approximations. They cannot possibly capture reality in all its complexity and fullness. As a result, they cannot possibly deliver perfect predictions of events. This is no less true of the physical sciences than it is of the social sciences.

The social sciences were the special object of Davis's concern. There, his bold contentions assumed their full force. If, strictly speaking, all theories were not true, what differentiated "good theories" from "poor ones"? Davis's answer was, "Some theories are more 'interesting' than others." This only raised the provocative question, What is it that makes a theory "interesting"?

For a theory to be interesting, it has to do a number of things. First, it has to raise to the surface a body of background assumptions that a significant group of people hold about some important aspect of the world. Second, the theory has to make the case that a set of completely opposite assumptions are more "plausible" than the initial ones.

Consider a simple example, the case of Sigmund Freud. Before Freud, the prevailing assumption was that the entire contents of the human mind were available for conscious inspection, and thus could be fully known by anyone who was willing to put in the time required to inspect one's own mind.[8] In other words, the assumption was that a person could have complete access to and thereby examine the full contents of his or her mind. After Freud, this assumption could no longer be held. Significant, perhaps vast, areas of the mind were unconscious and thus inaccessible. Indeed, significant thoughts were not available for conscious knowledge by the very person possessing those thoughts.

The upshot was that, in order for one mind to know itself, it had no choice but to enter into a deep and prolonged relationship with another mind, presumably one that was professionally trained—a counselor, psychiatrist, psychoanalyst, or therapist.

But Davis went even further. He made the shrewd observation that if someone merely replaced a few fundamental or sacred assumptions, and if the replacement assumptions did not challenge the initial ones strongly enough, then the most likely reaction was, "That's obvious!" In such situations, the opposite assumptions would be regarded by most people as trivial and not very interesting. At the other end of the spectrum, Davis noted with equally acute insight that if someone challenged in the strongest possible way all of a person's or a society's pet assumptions, then the reaction was, "That's absurd!"

For something to be considered "interesting," it had to challenge a person's underlying assumptions "strongly enough" to get one's attention and hold it. At the same time, one could not challenge the initial set of assumptions so strongly or completely that the challenge was rendered absurd. Thus, for something to be "interesting," it had to "whack" someone on the head enough to capture his or her attention, but not so strongly as to knock the person out.

The point of Davis's discussion for CM is as follows: At best, normal accidents are in the far end of the "interesting" region. But, to be sure, abnormal accidents are firmly in the "absurd" region. That is, the nature of the world has shifted profoundly. This is one of the reasons crises *are* crises, and why they are so difficult for most people to consider. In effect, something is a crisis if and only if it threatens to demolish *all* of our critical assumptions about a person, an organization, or even a society.

Concluding Remarks

The point of this chapter is certainly not that one can anticipate and think about every potential crisis. (Indeed, as the last chapter pointed out, the world is too fuzzy, uncertain, and imprecise for this ever to occur.) In fact, we can say with almost virtual certainty that this is *not* possible. On the other hand, it is possible to think about the unthinkable.

The purpose of thinking like a controlled paranoid is to help prepare the mind before horrendous acts occur by understanding how paranoids and terrorists think. The more horrific the act, the more this kind of thinking is absolutely necessary.

The more preparation that one has in thinking about the possibility of horrendous acts, the better one is able to cope with them (see Chapter Two). This does not mean that one has to accept such acts.

I want to end this chapter by going back to one of the prime assumptions that we have been considering throughout this book. If RB's top management fails to embrace the methods given in this chapter, then one of the prime charges that will be leveled against it is as follows:

You—management—failed to make the world safer; that is, RB has failed its employees, and its surrounding communities by not thinking like a controlled paranoid!

Notes

1. See Alistair Munro, *Delusional Disorder: Paranoia and Related Illnesses* (Cambridge, England: Cambridge University Press, 1999).
2. Ibid.
3. Monika Gattman, "Supernatural, Implantable Devices that Replace Defective Body Parts Not Only Take Over Where Nature Left Off, They Often Improve on the Original Design," *USC Health*, Fall 2003, pp. 4–9.
4. Robert Langer, "Where a Pill Won't Reach: Implanted Microchips, Embedded Polymers, and Ultrasonic Blasts of Proteins Will Deliver Next-Generation Medicines," *Scientific American*, 288, no. 4 (April 2003), pp. 50–58.
5. Ibid.
6. Gary Matsumoto, "Anthrax Powder: State of the Art?," *Science*, 302 (November 28, 2003), pp. 1492–1497.
7. Murray S. Davis, "That's Interesting! Towards a Phenomenology of Sociology and a Sociology of Phenomenology," *Philosophy of the Social Sciences,* 4 (December 1971), pp. 309–344.
8. See Steven A. Mitchell and Margaret J. Black, *Freud and Beyond: A History of Modern Psychoanalytic Thought* (New York: Basic Books, 1995).

CHAPTER SIX

Challenge 6

Right Transfer (Aesthetic IQ): Down with the Old; Design and Implement New Organizations

General Motors Corp. will rename its Buick LaCrosse in Canada because the name for the car is slang for masturbation in Quebec, an embarrassed official with the U.S. auto maker said on Thursday. GM officials, who declined to be named, said it had been unaware that LaCrosse was a term for self-gratification among teachers in French-speaking Quebec.

—Reuter's News Service, October 22, 2003

National Security Advisor Condoleezza Rice, in testimony before the [9/11] Commission, said the failure to detect the Sept. 11 plot was in large part a result of "structural" weaknesses in the intelligence community, particularly legal and other barriers that prevented the F.B.I., the C.I.A., and other agencies from sharing information fully . . .

But the disclosures by the 9/11 Commission suggested that the F.B.I.'s failures before the terrorist attacks were worse—and more systemic—than previously acknowledged, despite a steady stream of already embarrassing revelations over the last 2½ years.

—John Meyer, "Hearing Focuses Harsh Light on FBI: A Spike in Ominous Intelligence Leading Up to 9/11 Went Unshared, Even Within the Bureau," *Los Angeles Times*, April 10, 2004, pp. A-1, A-19

While American troops were still in Somalia [General Gordon Sullivan, the Army Chief of Staff in the early 90s] successfully pushed for the creation of a Peacekeeping Institute on the campus of the Army War College. The institute would both teach and help formulate a doctrine of peacekeeping. It offered two elective courses, in peacekeeping operations and negotiation—both always oversubscribed—to the 350 Lieutenant Colonels who went through the War College every year. Meanwhile, the Pentagon created a new Office of Peacekeeping and Peace Enforcement Policy.

—James Traub, "Peacekeeping: Can It Ever Be Made to Work?," *New York Times Magazine,* April 11, 2004, pp. 34–35

The Argument

1. The history of American corporations demonstrates that they have been built on two powerful, but faulty assumptions: (a) An organization is a machine—that is, it can be broken apart indefinitely into separate departments, functions, and divisions. In short, it is nothing more than the sum of separate, self-standing, and isolated silos (see Chapter Four); (b) As new problems and issues arise, new departments, functions, and silos can be added to the basic design without disturbing it in any essential way.
2. Both of these assumptions are wrong, dead wrong!

Chapters Four and Five have examined the failures of conventional thinking and their impact on crisis management (CM). This chapter discusses how the basic design of institutions that was established in the early twentieth century is largely responsible for the inability of today's organizations to respond to major crises.

The Design of General Motors

In 1963, the seminal business autobiography of one of General Motors' (GM) first CEOs, Alfred P. Sloan, *My Years with General Motors,*[1] was published. It was, and still is, one of the most important books in the short history of CM. While it became an instant bestseller—it was one of the first "business blockbusters"—it was never recognized nor referred to as a book on CM. Although the word *crisis* occurs regularly and repeatedly throughout Sloan's text, it is thereby puzzling that it was not listed in the index. Undoubtedly this was because it was not until some nineteen years later that the field of CM was invented. The 1982 tampering of Tylenol capsules in a suburb of Chicago is generally recognized as the starting point for crisis management.[2]

Sloan's autobiography makes it abundantly clear that, although it had undergone numerous modifications, the design of GM that emerged in the 1920s remains essentially unchanged today. Furthermore, since Sloan's design was widely adopted by other American businesses, as well as government agencies, it applies to them also. Most important, since this design was the direct response to a particular set of crises that GM faced in the 1920s, *today's organizations are largely the result of crises experienced some eighty-two years ago!* No wonder that our current organizations have poor responses to contemporary crises such as sexual harassment, workplace violence, and terrorism. In short, today's organizations attempt to respond to crises for which they were not designed.

Notice carefully that I am not saying that organizations have *not* changed substantially during the twentieth century and early part of the twenty-first. They have. But despite all appearance of change, their underlying operations and design, and even more the mentality on which they are based, are essentially the same. In short, today's organizations are rooted in the machine-age thinking of the nineteenth and early twentieth centuries. (Recall that we discussed the assumptions of the machine age and its reactions to problems in Chapter Four.)

GM's Four Major Crises

In the late 1910s and the early 1920s, the four crises that GM faced were: (1) extreme ups and downs in the general economy (what else is new?); (2) gaining control of its huge inventory of cars (believe it or not, GM didn't know how many cars it was producing annually); (3) getting accurate and timely sales data from GM's dealers (GM didn't know how many cars it was actually selling); and (4) getting the various car divisions to share their revenues with the central corporation on a continuing basis.

Unlike far too many of today's CEOs, Sloan did not opt for short-term, temporary, solutions. He and his colleagues fashioned and pushed through long-term, permanent changes in the overall operating structure of GM. The most important change was the creation of the Finance Committee at the very top of the corporation.

While Sloan did not *invent* the field or the discipline of Finance, he did establish the world's first Finance Department. This fact alone justifies a brief history of CM. Unfortunately, far too many people assume—quite erroneously—that finance departments have been around since time immemorial. They have not.

The job of the Finance Committee was twofold: to get an accurate picture of the total revenues and expenses of the corporation; and, even more important, to foster long-term economic planning so that the corporation could gain control over its financial destiny. That this structure worked so well is one of the reasons GM became and, until relatively recently remained, the world's largest corporation. (In the 1960s, GM had 50 percent of the U.S. car market. By the end of the late 1990s, this market share had shrunk to 25 percent, an "unthinkable" crisis of major proportions.)

The distinctive quality of Sloan's attitude and responses cannot be overemphasized. Even though the fluctuations in the economy were temporary, Sloan was not shortsighted. He did not rationalize the way far too many of today's executives do after a crisis has passed: "Whew, that's over! Let's put it behind us and get back to 'business as usual.' Let's not wallow in what's depressing."

Of course, it can be argued that without adequate financial controls there would be no corporation at all. By definition, anything that threatens a corporation's financial base will be a concern of the first order. Financial problems call for drastic, even permanent, solutions. A financial crisis of any kind will automatically receive and command the attention it deserves.

But while this may be true, it is also a fact that today's crises pose challenges that Sloan and his colleagues could never have envisioned. Indeed, today's crises have the potential of wreaking extreme financial havoc (e.g., the Ford/Firestone debacle, Enron) and, in some cases, destroying the corporation (e.g., the businesses that were housed in the World Trade Center). As recent history showed with the demise of Arthur Andersen, it is possible for large organizations to go out of existence as the result of a major crisis. The $64 billion dollar questions thus become: (1) What will it take for today's organizations to realize that they need to change their basic operating structures so that they can respond effectively to crises far beyond those ever experienced or envisioned by Sloan and his colleagues? and (2) What new operating structures are required if today's organizations are to respond effectively to the crises they face?[3]

The Need for Crisis Leadership

Although Sloan didn't use the term "infrastructure," he did put into place a deliberate structure for managing the crises of his day. The importance of this action is best seen by means of the following: If today we were to walk into any corporation and inquire whether it had a department specifically dedicated to finance, at best we would be met with looks of bewilderment. The very question would be enough to certify that one was "unbalanced." However, if we were to walk into the same corporation and inquire whether there was a dedicated infrastructure for CM or, better yet, crisis leadership, we would also be met with looks of bewilderment. The two "looks" would not be the same.

An organization would be considered crazy if it did *not* have a Finance Department, as well as a senior executive for finance. In the case of crisis leadership, however, we would be considered crazy if we thought that such a department was necessary.

Far too many executives believe that adding infrastructure for crisis leadership is tantamount to adding another layer of corporate bureaucracy. This is not the case. All structures are not the same. They are not all inherently bad. For instance, there is all the difference in the world between structures that *enable* and those that stifle and strangle an organization. Enabling structures are not the same as bureaucratic ones.[4]

I am not thereby calling for adding more bureaucratic layers to an organization. Instead, I am calling for the integration or synthesis of appropriate structures that will allow global corporations to give proper autonomy to local operating units. This is because local units know local markets better than bureaucrats ensconced at headquarters. Yet, global corporations must have the machinery for responding to crises that affect the whole organization.

Don't confuse an *integrated* design, which is critical to crisis leadership, with one that is *centralized* and *bureaucratic,* which is typical of risk management. Integration is not the same as a primitive fusion of business functions. There is no getting around the fact that today's organizations are global—period! This means that a crisis in one locale can swiftly escalate to become a crisis for an entire organization. Therefore, both globally integrated and locally responsible structures are needed.[5]

An Example: The Coca-Cola Company's "Belgium Crisis"

Consider the "Belgium crisis" that the Coca-Cola Company experienced a few years ago. Briefly, the health authorities in Belgium received numerous and mounting complaints that children were becoming sick after drinking Coca-Cola. The complaints claimed that the cans and the drink smelled and tasted "funny." Unfortunately, the Coca-Cola Company dismissed the complaints as "merely psychological."

Technical analyses confirmed that there was nothing wrong with the products from a quality standpoint—therefore, the problem had to be "in the minds" of consumers. By the time that the Coca-Cola Company realized that no amount of technical information or "gobbly-gook" was going to persuade consumers to stop feeling sick, they had a full-blown crisis on their hands. In addition, the Belgium Minister of Health became so infuriated at the Coca-Cola Company's delayed response that he ordered all cans of Coca-Cola to be pulled from the shelves of all stores in Belgium. But the crisis did not stop there. To distance themselves from Coca-Cola, McDonald's, one of the Coca-Cola Company's largest partners, stopped serving Coca-Cola in all of its outlets.

As a result of his poor handling of the crisis, the CEO of Coca-Cola, M. Douglas Ivester, was fired. Unfortunately, this was not enough to stave off the damage that was being done to Coca-Cola's reputation worldwide.

The Chief Crisis Officer

Because finance departments have been around for eighty years, we believe that a formal financial function has always been present. However, if we were able to transport ourselves back in time to when Sloan was CEO of GM, we would realize that his proposals for meeting the crises of his times were no less radical than ours are today.

If today's organizations are to respond effectively to the crises they face, then they will need a chief crisis officer. There is no longer any excuse for every organization's *not* having a full-time, senior executive in charge of the crisis capabilities of his or her organization. But organizations need something even more radical. They need world-class crisis learning and signal detection centers. Among the major purposes of such centers is the monitoring of early warning signals for potential crises and unthinkables. Of course, this early detection cannot be accomplished with any guarantee of perfection. But this limitation does not relieve us of the responsibility of doing everything humanly possible to prevent a crisis. To borrow an analogy from the field of medicine, because we cannot treat successfully all of the factors responsible for heart disease, this does not relieve us from attacking each of them as aggressively as we can.

A major function of crisis learning centers is to study the patterns associated with past crises, to distill critical lessons from these patterns, and to ensure that the organization puts these lessons into practice so that the potential for crises is lowered considerably. Understanding these patterns involves learning when, where, and why certain crises have occurred, and what, if anything, could have lowered the chances of their occurrence, as well as their impacts. Although it is clearly impossible to prevent all crises, being prepared for *any* crisis speeds up recovery time. Being prepared also lowers dramatically the economic costs of a crisis, and also lessens the psychological impact.

Moving Crisis Leadership to Center Stage

We cannot expect to win new wars with old tactics. Crisis leadership has to move from the periphery of organizations to their very center. This means that all organizations need to be redesigned around crisis leadership. A key element of this new design is the crisis learning center.

Flawed by Design

In *Flawed By Design*,[6] UCLA political scientist Amy Zegart has argued convincingly that government agencies have fared no better than private corporations when it comes to managing major crises. Zegart has shown why U.S. government agencies charged with monitoring terrorist and intelligence information were flawed from their very inception—that is, by deliberate design. Thus, the CIA, FBI, FAA, and other agencies were "deliberately designed" *not* to share information in a timely and efficient fashion.

This was not done out of malicious intent. It was done out of understandable fears that the concentration of terrorist information in a single government agency would lead to abuses of power by the U.S. government. It was also the result of political fighting among the U.S. House of Representatives, the Senate, the president, and the various branches of the armed forces over control of information regarding terrorism. In short, the fight was over who would have control over what. The end result is a complete mishmash of agencies charged with collecting, analyzing, and disseminating intelligence to the right governmental units and persons, so that effective action can be taken in a timely fashion.

Most critical of all, the government's design for handling intelligence on terrorism no longer works. As a consequence, Zegart argues that basic government agencies have to be fundamentally redesigned so that they can function in an integrated manner. They certainly do not need to be fused into a single, central, bumbling, bureaucratic agency.

Concluding Remarks

Many executives at well-managed companies secretly believe that they can work their way out of a crisis when the time comes without having a plan beforehand. As a result, they treat crisis preparation as a less-than-useful scenario-planning exercise that, if it must, can be conducted sporadically. That attitude won't change until companies create organizational mechanisms that make CM a top priority.

Crisis planning has usually been regarded as part of risk management, which is handled by the controller's office. Or it's been relegated as a lesser responsibility of the human resources or administration department. Either way, it ends up being less than half a job for someone two or three levels below the CEO. To elevate the function, proactive companies have created a CM office or crisis center, whose head reports to the CEO, COO, or CIO.

A crisis center has three responsibilities. First, it designs the company's crisis portfolio, which consists of at least one possibility from each crisis family, and draws up prevention and response plans for each crisis. Some centers have appointed champions for each type of crisis who help develop scenarios and strategies for that type of emergency. In addition, the crisis center prepares for the possibility that one calamity might trigger off another, or that more than one crisis might erupt simultaneously—scenarios that are becoming increasingly common.

Second, the crisis center stays on the alert for the signals that inevitably precede a crisis, amplifies them, and distributes warnings to the right executives in the company. By integrating signals that come from, say, different parts of the world, organizations can possibly detect problems before they blow up. For example, Ford might have averted the Firestone tire crisis in 2000 if it had paid attention to reports of its tires coming apart in Saudi Arabia and Venezuela. Instead, it wasn't until the crisis erupted in the United States that Ford put together a 500-person taskforce to see if it faced similar problems elsewhere in the world.

Finally, it is the crisis center's responsibility to develop real crisis capabilities rather than paper plans. It conducts regular audits and training exercises, installs mechanisms to contain crises, and develops programs to help executives communicate with internal and external stakeholders during a crisis. It is also the crisis center's responsibility to identify or set up alternate work sites in case the company's offices and plants are destroyed. The latter isn't as far-fetched as it once seemed for, as author Salman Rushdie said as long ago as November 1990, "One of the extraordinary things about human events is that the unthinkable becomes thinkable."

Postscript

As innovative as the chief crisis officer and the concept of a crisis learning center are, they do not go far enough. They do not recognize the idea of quantum organizations. The idea of quantum organizations derives from quantum mechanics.

In the world of quantum mechanics, which describes the behavior of atoms and their constituent parts at the subatomic level, particles are no longer rigid objects with fixed boundaries. In other words, Newtonian physics does not work at the microscopic level. Instead, at the quantum level, objects become extremely fuzzy. Indeed, they *are* fuzzy. Instead of being fixed objects in known positions, they are described by probability functions that postulate that an object has only a certain probability of being in a particular place at a particular time. In this way, both the objects and their boundaries are highly permeable.

Ralph Kilmann has extended this intriguing idea to organizations.[7] The upshot is that there are not, and more important, there should not be rigid boundaries between the departments or the various businesses of an organization in the modern age (see Figure 3-3). Indeed, if every business is now in every other business, then every business function is in every other business function as well.

To say the least, the world is not yet organized in this way. Even worse, it does not recognize that it needs to be. Nonetheless, some organizations are beginning to approach the idea of quantum organizations with regard to security. They have approached the idea of a quantum organization through the concept of "distributed security." That is, security, or much more generally CM, is part of everybody's job. To incorporate this notion into RB would be, among many things, to add the concept of a crisis academy to Figure 3-3. In effect, every employee in the organization would be a fellow of the crisis academy.

As far as I am aware, no organization, public or private, for profit or not for profit, has patterned a crisis unit on the model of al Qaeda. Unfortunately, al Qaeda is one of the most innovative organizations existing today. If not on the quantum model, then certainly al Qaeda patterns itself on a biological model. That is, al Qaeda is composed of relatively autonomous, self-contained cells, each of which operates independently of the other. In this way, it is almost impossible to bring al Qaeda down, for there is no central headquarters or "central mind" in the organization. Again, to my knowledge, I know of no organization in the United States or Western Europe that has patterned its security, counterterrorism, or CM activities around this innovative design.[8]

Notes

1. Alfred P. Sloan, Jr., *My Years with General Motors* (New York: Doubleday, 1963).

2. See I. I. Mitroff and G. Anagnos, *Managing Crises Before They Happen: What Every Executive and Manager Needs to Know About CM* (New York: AMACOM, 2000); see also Thierry C. Pauchant and Ian I. Mitroff, *Transforming the Crisis-Prone Organization: Preventing Individual, Organizational, and Environmental Tragedies* (San Francisco: Jossey-Bass, 1992).
3. See P. S. Adler and B. Borys, "Two Types of Bureaucracy: Enabling and Coercive," *Administrative Science Quarterly*, 41 (1996), pp. 61–89; Ralph H. Kilmann, *Quantum Organizations: A New Paradigm for Achieving Organizational Success and Personal Meaning* (Palo Alto, Calif.: Consulting Psychologists Press/Davies-Black Publishing, 2001); see also Karl E. Weick, Kathleen M. Sutcliffe, and Robert E. Quinn, *Managing the Unexpected: Assuring High Performance in an Age of Complexity* (San Francisco, Calif.: Jossey-Bass, 2001).
4. See Kilmann, *Quantum Organizations.*
5. C. A. Bartlett and S. Ghoshal, "Beyond the M-Form: Toward a Managerial Theory of the Firm," *Strategic Management Journal*, 14 (1993, special issue), pp. 23–46; C. A. Bartlett and S. Ghoshal, "Managing Across Borders: New Strategic Requirements," *Sloan Management Review,* 1987, pp. 7–17.
6. Amy B. Zegart, *Flawed By Design: The Evolution of the CIA, JCS, and NSC* (Stanford, Calif.: Stanford University Press, 1999).
7. Kilmann, *Quantum Organizations.*
8. For further reading, see Weick and Sutcliffe, *Managing the Unexpected.*

CHAPTER SEVEN

Challenge 7

Right Soul (Spiritual IQ): Spirituality Is *The* Ultimate Competitive Advantage

The evolutionary biologist E. O. Wilson has decreed that you cannot tread the path of spirituality and the path of reason; you must choose between them.

—John Horgan, *Rational Mysticism: Dispatches from the Border Between Science and Spirituality* (New York: Houghton Mifflin, 2003), p.11

Creating artificial or didactic boundaries between thought and emotion obscures the experiential and neurobiological reality of their inseparable nature.

—Daniel J. Siegel, *The Developing Mind: How Relationships and the Brain Interact to Shape Who We Are* (New York: Guilford, 1999), p. 159

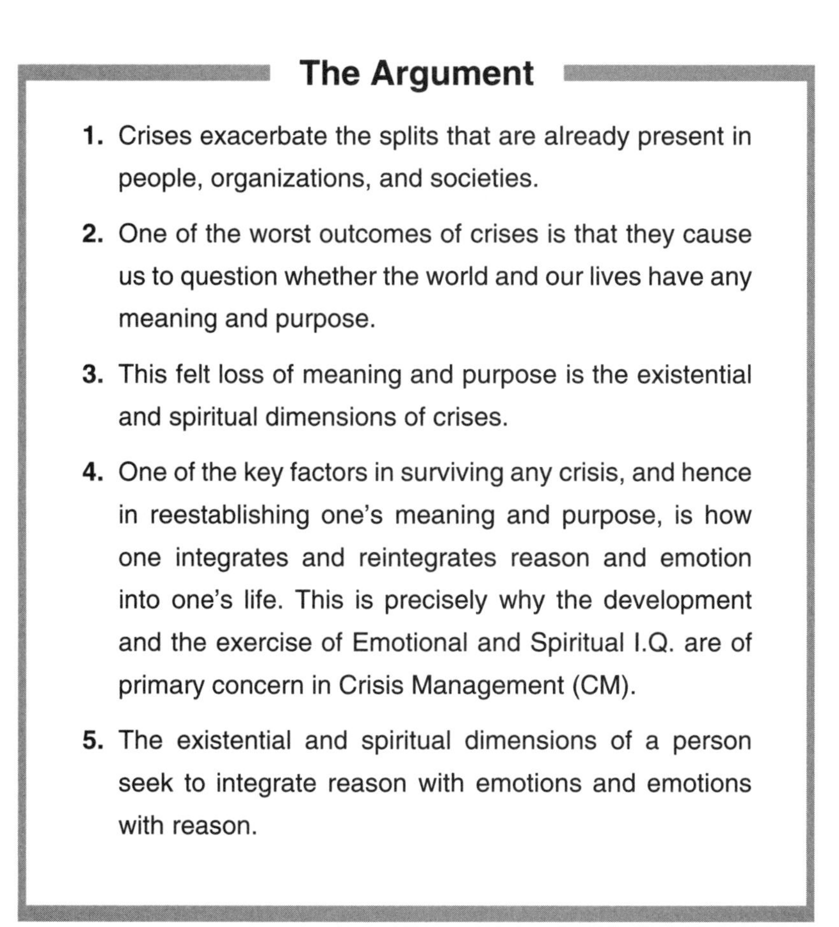

The Argument

1. Crises exacerbate the splits that are already present in people, organizations, and societies.
2. One of the worst outcomes of crises is that they cause us to question whether the world and our lives have any meaning and purpose.
3. This felt loss of meaning and purpose is the existential and spiritual dimensions of crises.
4. One of the key factors in surviving any crisis, and hence in reestablishing one's meaning and purpose, is how one integrates and reintegrates reason and emotion into one's life. This is precisely why the development and the exercise of Emotional and Spiritual I.Q. are of primary concern in Crisis Management (CM).
5. The existential and spiritual dimensions of a person seek to integrate reason with emotions and emotions with reason.

How Organizations Wound Us: The Spiritual and Existential Dimensions of Crises

To begin, one of the worst ways that organizations hurt and wound us is by reinforcing the fiction that the physical, the mental, and the spiritual exist in three separate realms and have nothing to do with one another. (As the first quotation to this chapter demonstrates, the Harvard evolutionary biologist E. O. Wilson believes that reason and spirituality not only *are* separable from one another, but that they *must* be separate.) To put it mildly, this is one of the greatest splits that has been perpetrated on the human condition. Crises exacerbate the splits that are already present in people, organizations, and societies. They increase whatever fears we had before a crisis.

Organizations, no less than individuals, are subject to such splits in their personalities. These splits affect not only their financial performance but also the number of crises they experience, and in many cases, the crises they cause. In turn, the number of crises an organization causes affects the financial and emotional well-being of not only those who work in the organization but larger society as well. For these reasons alone, we need to understand the splits that organizations foster, as well as their consequences.

Not only do individuals use defense mechanisms but organizations do as well. Organizations, no less than individuals, use splitting as a means of coping. By separating emotions from thinking, they ward off anxiety and other unpleasant feelings. Or at least, they operate under the fiction that they can manage feelings and emotions. For this reason, there is no more important task for crisis management than healing the split between thinking and feeling. Indeed, healing this rift is one of the prime concerns of spirituality, which transcends the dualism.

The Human and the Social Costs of Separating Reason from Emotion

The latest research in neurobiology and neurophysiology has given us new and very different portraits of the human mind. The constant interplay, as well as the interdependency between the so-called rational, cognitive aspects of the human mind and the so-called emotional aspects, are much stronger than previously imagined.[1] When we attempt to separate thought from emotion, we not only set up an artificial divide within ourselves but an internal war as well, a war that we cannot possibly win.

One of the reasons so many organizations are prone to major crises is that they emphasize the so-called rational aspects of the human mind to the exclusion of the so-called emotional aspects, or vice versa.[2] For instance, if one emphasizes the supposedly rational aspects of a crisis to the detriment of its emotional aspects, then like RB one will tend to prepare only for those crises that have a high probability of occurring *and* a high consequence associated with their occurrence. That is, one will not only use risk management (RM) but will believe also that RM is the basis of crisis management (CM). As a result, one will ignore not only certain types of crises, such as terrorism, which is extremely unpleasant to contemplate emotionally, but also the emotional and existential aspects of all other crises. As we shall see shortly, the emotional and existential are integral parts of spirituality.

Spirituality: The Constant Search for Meaning

In order to understand how crises perturb our basic sense of meaning, purpose, and justice in the universe, it is first necessary to have a deeper understanding of spirituality. Over the past five years, I have interviewed managers and executives with regard to spirituality in the workplace.[3] The interviewees were from all kinds of organizations. They included for profits as well as not-for-profits, divisions of government, and social service agencies. The primary purpose of these interviews was to ascertain what gives people meaning in their work and lives, and the relationship, if any, between the two. The interviews also explored much more sensitive issues such as the relationship of spirituality and religion to work.

To my knowledge, no other study has explored specifically how managers and executives *define* what religion and spirituality mean to them. While other studies have certainly examined the religious and spiritual practices of managers and executives, no one seems to have looked deeper into the underlying *meaning* of religion and spirituality for these managers.

The most important outcomes of the interviews were, first, the finding that people desperately want an opportunity to realize their potential as *whole* human beings, both on and off the job. Second, they want to work for ethical organizations. Third, they want to do interesting work. And while making money certainly is important, at best it is a distant fourth goal for most people.

No matter what question was asked, the answers given expressed people's intense desire to bring their whole person, or "complete package," to work. People were frustrated in having to leave significant parts of themselves at home. They were even more annoyed that anyone would even ask such a thing of them. Most people reported that they could bring only their brains to work, not their deepest feelings and emotions, let alone their souls. But this situation has the dire consequence that organizations do not reap the full creativity of their employees, and employees do not get the opportunity to develop themselves as whole persons.

Thus, the first split that organizations reinforce is that between a person's cognitive I.Q. and his or her emotional, ethical, and spiritual I.Q. In fact, one of the major indignities that people reported they suffer at work is enduring the fiction that their "cognitive parts" can be split from their "emotional, ethical, and spiritual parts."[4] In other words, this split is one of the major existential costs of working.

People especially want to develop and express their soul and spirit at work—the place where they spend the majority of their waking time. They are tired of being used and abused by organizations. They have had it with "all the BS, buzzwords, the endless parade of stupid fads, dumb tricks, and management gimmicks that really fool no one and accomplish nothing fundamental and long-lasting."[5]

A significant majority, up to 60 percent, made a sharp differentiation between religion and spirituality. Religion was viewed as dividing people through dogma and its emphasis on formal structure. Religion was also viewed as intolerant, close-minded, and excluding those who did not believe similarly. Spirituality, on the other hand, was viewed as both personal and universal at the same time. It was also perceived as tolerant, open-minded, and potentially inclusive. In other words, not all splits are regarded as bad by all people. Some splits, or distinctions, are seen as serving a greater good. Therefore, we have to distinguish between functional and dysfunctional splits. And though some splits are harmful or dysfunctional, not all splits are. To regard everything as either good or bad is to lose the power to make ethical distinctions and critical judgments.[6]

When the interviewees were asked for their definitions of spirituality and what meaning it had for their lives, everyone essentially had the same definition, whether they were religious or not: Spirituality is the intense feeling of not only being integrated as a whole person but also being connected with everything else in the universe. Spirituality Is the Ultimate Ground, the Supreme Guarantor, and the Fundamental Basis for ultimate meaning, purpose, and responsibility in people's lives.

Major crises disrupt not only people's prevailing definition of spirituality but, much more important, the intense feelings and emotions that lie behind that definition and constitute its essence. For instance, major crises almost always promote intense feelings of fragmentation. They cause us to feel disconnected with everything in our immediate lives, as well as the universe itself. They lead us to feel that the fundamental meaning and purpose of our lives has been seriously disrupted, if not destroyed. This disruption is the spiritual and existential dimension, or felt loss, that comes with virtually all major crises. It is, in fact, the definition of *major crisis.*

Everyone interviewed for this study felt strongly that if people and organizations were spiritual, and hence followed a "higher set of ethical principles," they could not disown the negative impacts of their actions, particularly those that harmed the physical and social environments. One cannot be spiritual if one produces dangerous or shoddy products, abuses employees, disowns the bad consequences of one's products and services , and so forth. In short, one could not be spiritual if one did not think and act *systemically.* In the context of CM, being spiritual requires one to practice a systemic, integrative form of CM—the very type that we have been discussing in this book.

Another significant finding was that organizations perceived as "more spiritual" or "had a greater spiritual orientation" were also perceived as significantly more profitable. Not only did they allow their employees to bring more of themselves to work but, as a result, both employees and the businesses were able to "develop ethically" to a much greater degree. Spirituality was perceived as the only true and lasting competitive advantage. The vast majority of those interviewed felt strongly that if organizations wanted to be successful, they had no choice but to become spiritual.

To prevent misunderstanding, I need to make clear that nearly all of the people interviewed believed strongly that spirituality had to be practiced for its own sake—that is, not for financial gain—if it were to be successful. If one practices spirituality primarily for financial or instrumental gain, then neither spirituality nor financial gain will result. Even if financial gain didn't result, the interviewees would consider the organization "successful" if managed with "greater ethical principles in mind."

The Split Between Thinking and Emotion

I recently had the opportunity to repeat my study of spirituality in the workplace with additional organizations. The results shed even more light on why organizations have difficulty avoiding major crises.

The results revealed that there were sharp and crucial differences between how men and women "organize their minds" or their "mental spaces." When men and women were asked which parts of themselves they could bring to work, both men and women reported that they could bring significantly more of their brains—that is, their cognitive intelligence—to work than they could their emotions—that is, feelings, soul, and so on. Here's where the similarities ended.

When sophisticated statistical techniques were used to analyze the data, they revealed that men and women organize their thoughts and their feelings very differently from one another. Whereas men generally split their thinking—their left brains—from their emotions—their right brains—women do not. Men's "mental space" is sharply split, organized into two separate and independent dimensions—that is, thinking or reasoning versus emotions and feelings. To visualize this, view thinking as at 90 degrees—a right angle—to feeling. However, the results also revealed clearly that women had only one dimension! In other words, their thinking and their feelings were organized into one dimension!

This difference is profound. Whereas men generally compartmentalize, fragment, and do not integrate their thoughts with their feelings—in short, they split their thinking from their emotions—women do exactly the opposite. Whereas men have a more fragmented or split view of the world, women have a more integrated view.

Of course, these results do not mean, or they should not be interpreted as implying, that *all* women and *all* men in *all* institutions organize their mental spaces in the same way. As we know from innumerable studies, there are wide variations across and within genders, races, ethnic groups, organizations, institutions, and societies. It is more accurate to say that some men tend to fragment or to split their mental space into two dimensions, and some men do not. What is important is not the differences between the genders, but the differences between people who have a fragmented view of the world and those who have an integrated one. (Nonetheless, it is extremely interesting that *Time* magazine's persons of the year for 2002 were three women: Cynthia Cooper of WorldCom, Coleen Rowley of the FBI, and Sherron Watkins of Enron. All three women blew the whistle on their employers.[7])

The results are of more than academic interest. When the integrators and fragmenters or compartmentalizers were compared on other dimensions, the differences were equally sharp. Those who had an integrated view of the world tended to experience much less joy from their work than those who had a fragmented view. At the same time, those who had an integrated view reported that they were more depressed at work. Thus, compartmentalization and integration have their plus as well as their minus sides.

If a person has a more integrative view of the world, then he or she is more likely to expect more from work. If a person's expectations regarding work are not met, then he or she experiences less joy at work and is likely to feel more depressed. On the other hand, if a person has a compartmentalized or fragmented view of the world, then he or she is less likely to expect more from work and as a result will experience less depression.

The moral of the story is not that we should expect less from our work so that we will be less depressed. Instead, if we have an integrated view of the world, then organizations need to change radically to more fully meet the needs of their employees. Organizations also need to change so that they can get more from their employees. Integrated organizations require integrated people, and vice versa. It is unrealistic to expect integrated people to feel able and willing to display their "full selves" in organizations that are not equipped to respect and nurture them.

The Futility of Separating Feelings from Thoughts

The previous findings give us a true portrait of the human and social "costs" of separating reason from feelings and emotions. Indeed, my follow-up studies on spirituality in the workplace revealed the futility of trying to separate one's feelings from one's so-called rational thoughts. Even though the males in these organizations had predominantly a fragmented view of the world, nonetheless they could not always keep their feelings and emotions at bay. It was clear from the statistical results that the two dimensions into which males were dichotomizing the world were not, strictly speaking, pure or uncontaminated. A strong influence from the opposite side of their brains crept in and smudged the purity of both "pure thinking" and "pure emotions." Every dimension of thinking includes an element of feeling, and vice versa. But this doesn't mean that we are aware of this.

To understand why it is so difficult for many people, but especially men, to acknowledge emotion, let alone integrate it with their thinking, we have to turn to a field that treats the deeper parts of the human mind:

> Based on his own life and his clinical work as a psychiatrist, [Carl] Jung observed that young men normally suppressed their fear, pain, and neediness, dismissing these emotions as "feminine." Cast out of conscious awareness, the feelings go underground. But they are too powerful to be eliminated, so they surface in mid-life, demanding their due. Research from around the world confirms Jung's insights. As men age, they become more emotionally expressive, sensitive to relationships, and open about their fears and needs. Men move away from heroic stoicism and learn to honor the feminine. . . . Expressing emotions is difficult for men, admitting fears and doubts even more painful, and acknowledging feelings of dependence and the need for nurturing, downright shameful. Not surprisingly, many men seek therapy to sort out the confusing issues that arise when they grapple with their feminine side.[8]

Dealing with emotions—indeed, even acknowledging them in the first place—is one of the most important struggles that takes place in every person's life. It is especially difficult and painful for men to acknowledge, let alone to deal with, their emotions. And yet, if we do not deal with emotions, we and our organizations remain underdeveloped. Dealing with the whole person and the whole organization is vital.

Integrating Thought with Emotion: How Benetton-Turkey Dealt with a Major Crisis

Unfortunately, there are very few examples of organizations that successfully integrate thought and emotion. For this reason, I want to use an example that I have cited in a previous book. This is the case of Benetton-Turkey.[9]

About six years ago, my wife and I had the pleasure of visiting Istanbul, Turkey. While we were there, I talked with several CEOs regarding recent crises that they and their organizations had experienced. The most interesting was Benetton-Turkey. For over twenty years, the Turkish majority and the Kurdish minority have been at war. The Kurds want to set up their own ethnic state. As is so often the case, both sides have resorted to violence to control the outcome. Under the leadership of Kurdish rebel Abdullah Ocalan, or Apo as he is known, 30,000 Turks have been killed. In retaliation, untold numbers of Kurds have been imprisoned, tortured, and killed.

For years, Apo lived as a hunted man with a heavy price on his head. As the Turks were finally closing in on him, he fled to Moscow. Given the thaw in the cold war, Moscow was not anxious to receive him. As a result, he fled to Italy, where he was welcomed warmly by the Italian Communist Party and, unofficially, by the Italian government.

When the Turkish government demanded that Apo be extradited, the Italian government refused, citing the fact that Turkey believes in the death penalty to which Italy is vehemently opposed. When Turkey promised to rescind the death penalty, Italy still refused to release Apo.

The reaction in Turkey was immediate. The Turkish people took to the streets in thousands to protest against Italy and the Italian businesses that had subsidiaries in Turkey. Italian flags were burned. In addition, the demonstrators threatened to boycott Italian products and attack Italian stores and products such as Benetton, Ferrari, and Perelli. In short, the feeling was one of massive betrayal: the Turkish people had been betrayed by the Italians.

As soon as the protests began against Italian subsidiaries, most of the companies reacted predictably and defensively. They took out newspaper ads to the effect that the Turkish people should differentiate between Italian parent companies and Turks who operated them. In other words, the ads presented "logical and rational arguments"—that is, cognitive reasons—as to why the Turks who operated Italian businesses should not be seen as betrayers. To the people in the streets the ads were nonsense. Unfortunately, many corporate executives assume that the general populace thinks as they do—that is, as corporate executives.

Since corporate executives are rewarded for thinking in terms of the "boxes" on their organization charts, they assume that everyone else will think this way as well. As obvious as their view of the situation may have been to the executives, not all Turkish citizens are executives, let alone executives of an Italian company.

There was one Italian-based company that did not respond in a knee-jerk fashion. It not only *thought* the unthinkable, but it *did* the unthinkable as well. That company was Benetton-Turkey. Benetton-Turkey faced the destruction of its stores, property, and substantial harm to its employees and customers. As a result, Benetton-Turkey's top corporate executives met with unprecedented concern and speed. Composed of its President, Head of Public Affairs, and Head of Corporate Finance, the company's top "corporate response team" decided that they should react emotionally to the situation, not merely rationally or cognitively. They took out ads that sided *emotionally* with the Turkish people. The ads proclaimed: "First and foremost, we are Turks too! Our first allegiance and loyalty is to Turkey! We feel the same way that you do towards the Italians!"

Benetton-Turkey's top executives went even further. The next step was one of sheer brilliance. It demonstrates what most companies are unable to feel emotionally, and as a result, are unable to do in the heat of a major crisis.[10] It illustrates precisely the differences between cognitive and emotional I.Q. Benetton-Turkey went to the heart of its hard-won, highly visible, and identifiable corporate logo.

Over the years, Benetton has developed some of the most creative, attention-getting ads of any corporation. Because of its forceful, no-holds-barred approach, many of these ads have been controversial. At the heart of its corporate identity—its logo—is the notion of The United Colors of Benetton. This is meant to refer to the unification and integration of all people, everywhere. Benetton-Turkey reasoned that if it was to demonstrate its emotional affinity with the Turks against Italy, then it had to take action that was not only clear-cut but symbolic: it removed the colors from its logo, at least in Turkey! Likewise, the company proclaimed loudly and clearly, in highly visible and prominent ads, that until the situation with Italy was settled, black wreaths would hang on the storefronts of all Benetton stores in the country. All of the mannequins in its store windows would be dressed in black, indicating that the company was in a state of mourning, at least until the situation was resolved.

The response was instantaneous and overwhelming. The Turkish public responded so positively, and with so much emotion, that notes and poems were taped to Benetton storefront windows, indicating the public's deep and widespread support for the company. The notes and poems proclaimed that the public viewed Benetton-Turkey as a victim as well. It certainly was not the villain. The company had been betrayed as well by the Italian government and people.

But before they put wreaths on the storefronts, Benetton-Turkey's executives carefully checked with their store managers.

All of the managers enthusiastically endorsed the plan of temporarily taking the colors out of Benetton.

To further indicate the depth and sincerity of their support, Benetton-Turkey's executives also decided that, for at least the duration of the crisis, they would relieve some of the pressure on the stores. The boycotts had caused revenues to plummet, so the stores were excused indefinitely from meeting financial quotas. This had the additional effect of building trust and camaraderie between Benetton's store managers and its top executives, and this step alone is a primary illustration of emotional I.Q.

Because Benetton-Turkey's actions are still so completely out of the ordinary—"outside the box" of cognitive I.Q.—I cannot emphasize enough the cognitive and emotional creativity, as well as the riskiness, of their thinking and actions. Basically, Benetton-Turkey assumed that an act of defensiveness or caution would not save the day. Instead, the executives realized that they had to reverse a fundamental aspect of their corporate being. They took one of the most fundamental underpinnings of their corporate existence and identity and flipped it on its head—that is, their "colors." They did something that most businesses are almost totally unprepared to do. This is not to say that what they did was without considerable risk. But this type of thinking and action is precisely what makes a person, a company, an institution, and even a country's acts potentially "heroic."

It is interesting to compare Benetton's actions with those of other Italian-based companies in Turkey. The executives of these other companies assumed that they were the "true victims" of the situation, and thus they failed to acknowledge the real victims—both the Turkish majority and the Kurdish minority. Their response is one of the most prevalent ways that companies commit fatal mistakes. Instead of identifying with the true victims, they attempt to portray themselves as the victims. The result is that they end up becoming the villains.

The Benetton-Turkey story not only illustrates why emotional I.Q. is so important, but also precisely what it consists of. Most important, emotional I.Q. allows an organization to identify with the true victims of a situation and not to portray itself as the victim. That is, it allows an organization to overcome the natural tendency to employ the defense mechanism of splitting.

The Lack of Emotional Intelligence

If they even perform a stakeholder analysis, most managers and corporate executives perform a *cognitive* stakeholder analysis.[11] They typically analyze the so-called rational interests of stakeholders, such as their economic power, access to and control of information, and so on. Very rarely do they examine, let alone systematically examine, the emotional needs of stakeholders.

I cannot emphasize too strongly that it is emotional intelligence—and more often than not, its lack—that is key in *all* crisis situations. The emotional I.Q. allows a person to identify and respond appropriately to the emotional needs and concerns of the wide range of stakeholders that constitute all normal business and crisis situations. And it is precisely the emotional I.Q. that helps in avoiding acts of betrayal or in healing them whenever they occur.

One of the most conspicuous examples of a lack of emotional I.Q. is the frequent demand of many executives that consumers understand business from their standpoint. This faulty form of role reversal shows how the unconscious, emotional needs of executives take precedence over the needs of their consumers. Make no mistake about it. This role reversal is a primary case of the betrayal of consumers by corporate executives.

The "Firestone/Ford" Tire Crisis

Consider the "Firestone/Ford" tire crisis as another example. A prominent aspect of this tire crisis was the repeated assertion by both Firestone and Ford officials that, from a statistical standpoint, it is difficult to locate defective tires. Indeed, this is a constant "defense" given in most crises. In essence, it is a statistical argument: namely, the vast majority of tires or other products are safe; it is only a tiny fraction of products that are unsafe. Therefore, defects are rare, aberrations.

However, why should customers accept the statistical difficulties of locating hundreds of defective tires out of a total production of millions? While this corporate viewpoint may make sense from a cognitive standpoint, from an emotional perspective it merely heaps further insult upon death and injury.

Consumers are *not* statisticians, especially when they and their loved ones have been seriously injured or killed. This corporate attitude is one of the very worst instances of a *lack* of emotional I.Q. It presupposes that customers not only can but *ought* to put aside emotional concerns in favor of supposedly more legitimate cognitive or rational concerns. Yet this contention is absolutely preposterous. The failure to understand and respond appropriately to the emotional needs of consumers only yields consumer boycotts or rejection of a product as well as an organization. If executives fail to respond appropriately to the emotional needs of the stakeholders, then they have betrayed the very people they purport to serve, striking at the deepest layers of their being.

Unfortunately, the Firestone/Ford crisis is full of examples showing a failure to respond properly to the emotional needs of consumers. For instance, in bringing back the Explorer, Ford chose to use in its ads the insulting phrase "Reborn." How could they possibly bring back to life a machine that cost people their lives? This insensitivity says it all; it is typical of the whole Firestone/Ford crisis.

Three Types of Splits

Thus far, this chapter has discussed three types of splits to which both individuals and organizations are subject. These are:

1. Thinking or cognition versus feelings or emotions
2. Spirituality versus religion
3. Spiritual or religious concerns versus economic or worldly concerns

The thinking or the cognitive aspects of the human mind are often exalted and elevated over the feeling or emotional aspects. Cognition is idealized and feeling is demonized. At the same time, this split is experienced as self-betrayal, since it promotes a fundamental disharmony between the two halves of our deepest selves.

Spirituality is often idealized and religion is, in effect, demonized. Because of the fear that spirituality will lead to an "official company religion," and because of the failure historically to develop ways of fostering spirituality at work in ways that will not encroach on individual beliefs, organizations generally split their ethical and spiritual impulses from their economic ones. Thus the economic sphere is elevated and idealized while the spiritual sphere is shortchanged and even demonized.

Proactive Versus Reactive Organizations

Recall from Chapter One that organizations can generally be divided into two broad types with regard to their CM behavior and performance: proactive and reactive. Recall that proactive organizations anticipate and prepare for a larger number and wider variety of crises than those that they have already experienced (see Table 3-1). In contrast, reactive organizations prepare for a smaller number of crises than the ones that they have experienced. Thus, an easy way to differentiate between these two is to subtract the number of crises an organization has experienced from those that it is prepared for. This number is positive for proactive organizations, and negative for reactive.

As we also noted in Chapter One, the difference between these two types of organizations extends far beneath their surface behavior. Proactive organizations' operations operate by the ethical principle "Do no harm even to a single person."

This principle permeates their culture and business practices. As a result, it leads proactive organizations not only to take safety considerations extremely seriously but to take other programs such as Total Quality Management, Environmentalism, and the like seriously as well.

In contrast, reactive organizations operate by the ethical principle "Do the greatest good for the greatest numbers of people." Proactive organizations are guided largely by an ethical orientation that says "Do the right things irrespective of their costs." In contrast, reactive organizations are guided by the principle "Do what is right, but if and only if it is cost-effective."

As noted in Chapter One, while reactive organizations are guided almost entirely by cost considerations, they are substantially less profitable than proactive organizations as indicated by their R.O.A.s! Effective CM and ethics not only go hand in hand but together they pay off handsomely. In a word, they are good for business. These results should make business school faculties and executives give serious reconsideration to the value of business ethics. Ethics is *not* separable from CM—it is an integral component of effective CM.

The Link Between Betrayal and CM

Recall from Chapter Two that every major crisis is experienced as an act of betrayal. Table 7-1 shows the particular kinds of betrayal associated with each of the major types of crises (see Table 3-1).

In the case of Enron, multiple acts of betrayal occurred simultaneously. In this sense, the betrayal was experienced as, and was, systemic. The individual acts not only occurred simultaneously but reinforced one another. The end result was an entire culture of betrayal.

Perhaps the most basic kind of betrayal falls under the category "Human Resources." In this case, top management failed to devote adequate resources to the protection of the organization. In addition, top management erected, in effect, a strict separation between the thinking and the feelings of people in the organization. Major emphasis was on the cognitive—that is, the economic and technical concerns—to the detriment of the feelings, ethics, and existential concerns of the organization.

These differences between proactive and reactive organizations are reflected in the basic assumptions corporations make about the world. These assumptions are shown in Tables 7-2 and 7-3. They are in effect "spiritual contracts" with regard to their employees and society. Not only are they different "spiritual contracts" but they are also different "social contracts." They are certainly "spiritual" in that all of the assumptions construct two different worlds of meaning.

Table 7-1. Major crises as major forms of betrayal.

Economic	Information	Physical (loss of key plants and facilities and products)	Human Resources
Top management failed to protect my retirement income and investments. Top management failed to provide true accounting information on the actual financials of the organization. Top management engaged in dubious, criminal, and unethical financial schemes and accounting practices. Top management deliberately falsified accounting and financial information.	Top management deliberately lied and falsified company documents. Top management deliberately falsified accounting and financial information.	Top management compromised on the amount of resources devoted to plant and company safety.	Top management implemented reward systems that actively promoted ruthless behavior—for example, Enron's infamous "rank and yank" evaluation system. Top management fostered a culture of corruption.

Reputation	Psychopathic Acts	Natural Disasters
Top management deliberately fostered a Crisis Prone culture which ultimately sullied the reputation of the company.	Top management engaged in sociopathic behaviors.	Top management took advantage of different operating conditions around the world, and "cultural rules," to engage in unsafe practices that exacerbated the worst consequences of natural disasters; for instance, shoddy apartment buildings were built in various earthquake prone locations.

Table 7-2. Basic assumptions of proactive organizations.
1. One is obligated to make the world safe.
2. One is obligated to make the world good and just.
3. One is obligated to make the world stable and predictable.
4. One is obligated to limit betrayal.
5. One is obligated to reinforce the inherent goodness of people.
6. The organization is obligated to assume responsibility for its acts.
7. One is obligated to do everything possible to publicize advance warnings of crises.

Table 7-3. Basic assumptions of reactive organizations.
1. One is obligated to make the world safe if and only if it is cost-effective.
2. One is obligated to make the world good and just if and only if it is cost-effective.
3. One is obligated to make the world stable and predictable if and only if it is cost-effective.
4. One is obligated to limit betrayal if and only if it is cost-effective.
5. One is obligated to reinforce the inherent goodness of people if and only if it is cost-effective.
6. The organization is obligated to assume responsibility for its acts if and only if it is cost-effective.
7. One is obligated to do everything possible to surface advance warnings of crises if and only if it is cost-effective.

The Entrepreneur as Anti-Hero

One split is especially ominous. The split pertains not only to organizations but also institutions and society as a whole, a topic that is discussed in Chapter Eight.

Seeing the entrepreneur as a heroic ideal, or anti-hero of Western, capitalistic society fosters an extremely dangerous, if not sociopathic, view of the world, especially when it is combined with a consequentialist, reactive organization. The entrepreneur is entitled to operate as he or she does if we assume that the entrepreneur is warranted, if not obligated, to make the world *unsafe*. The entrepreneur not only is morally sanctioned but is expected to break the rules of society—in short, to be ruthless.[12]

The following is a typical expression of this notion:

> The job of the entrepreneur isn't to act prudently, to err on the side of caution. It's to err on the side of reckless ambition. It is to take the risk that the market allows him to take. What distinguishes a robust market economy like ours from a less robust one like, say, France's, is that it encourages energetic, ambitious people to take a risk—and that they respond to that encouragement. It encourages nerve, and that is a beautiful thing. As the business writer George Anders puts it, "The personality that allows you to be Jeff Bezos [the founder of Amazon.com] in the first place does not have a shut off valve." If it did, Amazon.com wouldn't exist.[13]

One finds this notion of the entrepreneur echoed repeatedly in various post-Enron analyses and commentaries.[14] In effect, Enron and Andersen are the prices that we pay for continuous innovation in capitalistic societies. According to this view, greed is not only cyclic but also inevitable. It is morally warranted and justified because of the creativity that the entrepreneur continually introduces into society.

This notion of the entrepreneur is as faulty as the notion once held with regard to slavery. It is akin to saying that slavery is "cyclic." Furthermore, it is as dubious as saying that slavery "served valuable economic interests" because it provided cheap, free labor. It is also equally faulty when it contends, as slavery once did, that it was rooted inevitably in the human condition. It was a fundamental part of human nature, and as such, was unalterable. Invoking the phrase "human nature" is the ultimate conversation stopper! If something is part of human nature, then by definition it is a supreme constraint; it cannot be gotten around.

If one accepts the proposition that the entrepreneur is morally entitled to make the world unsafe, then the entrepreneur is not only sanctioned but *expected* to commit betrayal! The underlying ethical position or theory of the entrepreneur does not even rise to the level of Utilitarianism, although there is certainly a strong element of that philosophy operating in entrepreneurship, namely "Get as much as you can for yourself." It is undergirded by the lowest form of ethical development—egoism, or "The only person that counts is me and me alone!" The portrait that emerges is of the entrepreneur as supreme egoist and sociopath. In Freudian terms, the entrepreneur lives out Freud's infantile fantasy of complete omnipotence without any regard for the feelings and considerations of others.

If you examine some of the recent, autobiographical accounts of Enron personalities, then this "reading" of Enron is justified.[15] For instance, Brian Cruver's autobiographical account reads more like a series of one-liners instead of the words of someone who is truly repentant of the misfortunes his participation in the Enron scandal caused everyone else. The entrepreneurial MBA, of which Cruver is a prime example, is caught up in a whirlwind of narcissistic excitement that was at the center of the storm known as Enron, and in the midst of that storm virtually anything was justified. Reading Cruver's account, one is left with the feeling that if Enron had not crashed, its actions would have been morally justified. For Cruver, the only real tragedy is that it eventually did crash.

Concluding Remarks

In the end, it is the split between the thinking or cognitive IQ and the emotional, ethical, and spiritual IQ that is responsible for most of the major crises we have experienced. There is no doubt that the people who were running Enron were intellectually smart, if not gifted in this regard. However, it is also clear that they were woefully lacking in ethical smarts. One is, in fact, reminded of the chilling line at the end of Arthur Koestler's book *The Sleepwalkers* with regard to the founders of modern astronomy—namely, they were "intellectual giants, but at the same time, moral dwarfs."[16]

A prime assumption is the following:

Reactive organizations fail to make the world safe by separating thinking from feeling, and by downplaying the existential, spiritual needs of humans.

If anything is central to the link between spirituality and CM, it is the material presented in Table 7-2. The Table 7-2 lists acknowledge that the world is not safe and it has never been so—

two assumptions that all crises call into question. Instead, the material directs us, if not commands us, to do everything in our power to make the world safer than we found it. This indeed may be the only action that can lead to restoration of trust in the world and in ourselves.

Proactive organizations restore meaning through their actions before, during, and after a major crisis. For instance, they allow people to grieve over the loss of their basic assumptions about the world, about themselves, and about the organization itself. In this way, they allow new assumptions to emerge.

Notes

1. Antonio R. Damasio, *Descartes' Error: Emotion, Reason, and the Human Brain* (New York: Avon, 1994).
2. David Collins, *Management Fads and Buzz Words: Critical-Practices Perspectives* (London: Rootledge, 2000).
3. Ian I. Mitroff, *A Spiritual Audit of Corporate America* (San Francisco: Jossey-Bass, 1999).
4. Daniel Goleman, *Emotional Intelligence: Why It Can Matter More Than I.Q.* (New York: Bantam, 1995).
5. See Marc Gunther, "God and Business," *Fortune*, July 16, 2001, pp. 59–80.
6. See Ken Wilber, *Integral Psychology: Consciousness, Spirit, Psychology, Therapy* (Boston: Shambhala Publications, 2000); see also Ken Wilber, *Boomeritis: A Novel That Will Set You Free* (Boston: Shambhala Publications, 2002.
7. See *Time*, December 30, 2002/January 6, 2003.
8. Allan Chinen, *Beyond the Hero: Classic Stories of Men in Search of Soul* (New York: Jeremy Tarcher, 1993), pp. 24–25.
9. Ian I. Mitroff with Gus Anagnos, *Managing Crises Before They Happen* (New York: AMACOM, 2001).
10. Ibid.
11. Ian I. Mitroff and Harold Linstone, *The Unbounded Mind: Breaking the Chains of Traditional Business Thinking* (New York: Oxford University Press, 1995).
12. "Thumped, But Don't Write Off American Capitalism Just Yet," *The Economist*, July 13, 2002, pp. 11–12; see also John Cassidy, "The World of Busi-

ness, The Greed Cycle: How Corporate America Went Out of Control," *The New Yorker*, September 23, 2002, pp. 64–77; Tony Mack, "The Other Enron Story: The Scandal-Plagued Giant Helped Spark Changes That Have Saved Businesses and Consumers Billion of Dollars in Energy Bills. Will Those Reforms Survive the Company?," *Forbes Magazine*, October 14, 2002, pp. 63–65.

13. Michael Lewis, "In Defense of the Boom: The Rush to Hang the Henry Blodgets of the World Is Rewriting History, and Obscuring What Was Great About the Nineties—and Handing the Economy Back to the Establishment," *New York Times Magazine*, October 27, 2002, p. 48.
14. "Thumped, But Don't Write Off American Capitalism Just Yet," *The Economist*, July 13, 2002, pp. 11–12; see also Cassidy, Op. Cit. and Mack, Op. Cit.
15. Brian Cruver, *Anatomy of Greed: The Unshredded Truth from an Enron Insider* (New York: Carroll & Graf, 2002).
16. Arthur Koestler, *The Sleepwalkers: A History of Man's Changing Vision of the Universe* (New York: Arkana, 1990).

CHAPTER EIGHT

When a Whole Society Is in Crisis, All of the Challenges Apply

The United States faces a trade off of time-honored American ideals: to preserve the most central of its founding principles, freedom, it must give up one of its founding myths, that of a people apart. America is now, ineluctably, part of a global community of its own making.

—Michael Hirsh, "Bush and the World," *Foreign Affairs*, September/October 2002, p.32

Americans generally see the world divided between good and evil, between friends and enemies, while Europeans see a more complex picture.

—Robert Kagan, *Of Paradise and Power: America and Europe in the New World Order* (New York: Knopf, 2003), p. 4

From the American perspective, exceptionalism means other nations have no particular right to deploy preventative strategies of their own.

—Benjamin R. Barber, *Fear's Empire: War, Terrorism, and Democracy* (New York: W.W. Norton, 2003), p. 98

The Argument

1. The deepest assumptions of societies are embodied in their fundamental myths and stories that explain how and why they came into being. They are, in fact, the very rationale for their being.
2. The myths and stories of a society both explain and justify the uniqueness of a people, a society, or a civilization.
3. The myths exist fundamentally to help a people or society cope with its anxieties and fears.
4. In addition to the horrific injuries and deaths of innocent civilians, crises such as 9/11 are traumatic because they invalidate the fundamental myths and stories of a people or society.
5. The final result of the collapse of a society's myths and stories is a deep existential and spiritual crisis. The crisis is experienced as a loss of meaning and purpose.

The September 11 attack brought home vividly that the United States is connected to the rest of the world in ways that are not always to its benefit. It also brought home the fact that no business exists in a vacuum. To understand the challenges facing American businesses today, it is necessary to understand not only those connections to the rest of the world but also the myths and stories of American society in which all American businesses are embedded.

The Importance of Myths

One of the most powerful ways to understand a society and its major institutions is to examine its central myths—the decisive, critical stories that it tells over and over to reassure as well as reaffirm itself, especially in times of crisis. These myths embody a society's fundamental assumptions about itself and its relationship to the rest of the world.

When those basic assumptions are shattered, an existential dilemma develops. Individuals, organizations, and institutions desperately search for and grab whatever other devices are available to prop them up. More often than not, these "devices" are other stories or myths. The components of such stories reflect the basic aspirations, fears, dreams, hopes, and struggles of the people.

The task of examining such fears, myths, stories, and values, particularly of U.S. society, has been aided immeasurably by the efforts of Robert Reich[1] and Rupert Wilkinson.[2] Each, in his own way, and apparently without knowledge of the other's efforts, has described four major themes that purport to capture the major fears and aspirations of U.S. society.

For Wilkinson, the primary values and driving forces can be captured in four major fears:

1. The fear of being owned
2. The fear of falling apart
3. The fear of falling away
4. The fear of winding down

For Reich, they are captured in four major myths or stories:

1. The mob at the gates
2. The rot at the top
3. The triumphant individual
4. The benevolent society

For Reich and Wilkinson alike, each of their four factors is so fundamental that over the entire course of U.S. history, Americans have (1) explained their condition, (2) defined and recognized their important problems, (3) sought solutions to them, and (4) framed important initiatives and programs in terms of them. While the particulars of the stories have varied dramatically over the course of our history, the underlying themes have not.

Wilkinson's Four Fears

The Fear of Being Owned

The fear of being owned is one of the earliest and perhaps the most basic and primitive of all the fears that Americans share. It derives from the major factor that caused our forefathers to leave Europe and immigrate to America: the long-suffered oppression at the hands of European nobility. Because of the depth to which this powerful fear is engrained in the American psyche, it has instilled a deep distrust of centralized big government, and all large institutions in general. For instance, it figured predominantly a few years ago in the debate regarding whether the United States needed an industrial policy—that is, a coherent and deliberately orchestrated plan at the national level to give support for promising industries. To carry out such a policy means, of course, concentrating in some central government agency the necessary intelligence, power, and resources to implement the plan. This fear also played a part in recent debates over whether to establish a Department of Homeland Security.

Because the fear of being owned is largely an unconscious one in the American psyche, it is difficult to address the merits versus demerits of an industrial policy on strictly rational grounds. The United States is now competing in a world economy against such players as Japan, South Korea, and Germany—players who have successful industrial policies because they believe that government must be a firm ally and not a feared adversary of business. This is still a foreign concept for Americans to accept. On the surface we can understand rationally that, in order to compete effectively, labor and management must join industry and government to forge close ties and overcome past adversarial relationships and mutual fears. This same set of considerations played a major role in the debate regarding the Department of Homeland Security—that is, whether it was needed, how it should be organized, and so on. All of these debates show that the fear of being owned is every bit alive.

The Fear of Falling Apart

The fear of falling apart captures all of the mutual antagonisms, conflicts, and strains that exist in a society as big, complex, divisive, and varied as ours. The fear of falling apart is that we will be overwhelmed by the problems of a complex society: crime, racial unrest, alcoholism, drugs, the homeless, the roller-coaster state of the economy, huge trade deficits, and, worst of all, the rise of worldwide terrorism. The fear is that our problems have become so big, so monumental, so impossible for anyone to state cogently, let alone treat effectively, that they will kill the American experiment. At the level of the individual, it is seen in our obsession with fads, the latest being the "health and exercise craze." At a personal level, the fear is symbolized by the desire to have a perfect face, perfect body, perfect family, perfect home, and perfect life, lest one disintegrate personally.

The Fear of Falling Away

The fear of falling away is the fear of abandoning the ideals of the American dream as laid down by the Founding Fathers. It is the fear of abandoning our spiritual heritage. In coming to America, our forefathers were not merely journeying to a new geographical or physical landscape. They were founding a new spiritual and moral landscape. America was to serve as a moral beacon to the world. The journey did not represent a beginning solely for the Pilgrims but, rather, for all of humankind. The uniqueness of the American experiment was that of starting a country, literally from scratch, untainted by the corruption of the Old World.

The Fear of Winding Down

The fear of winding down is the fear that we have lost the abiding and boundless energy of the people who settled the land. Of all of the fears, this one in particular is perhaps most easily recognized in everyday life. America is bristling with so much energy that it screams from its pores. As my colleague Warren Bennis reminds us, "in America there is plenty of action and activity everywhere, but precious little channeling of it into purposeful direction or accomplishment."

Given the tremendous upheaval that was experienced by mind and body in leaving the Old World, the perilousness of the journey, the frightful conditions during the first winters in the new land, plus the oppressive history from which we sprang, these fears make perfect sense. This is even easier to appreciate if we examine from a psychoanalytic perspective the dynamics behind each of the fears. We will do this after we have examined Reich's four myths, since the dynamics will be even easier to see.

Reich's Four Myths

The Mob at the Gates

The mob at the gates is the fear that unless America is constantly on guard, it will be overrun by the barbarians just outside our walls, who would rob us of our riches and destroy us. Given the strong moral and religious fervor of the Founding Fathers, as expressed in their establishing a nation to serve as a moral example for all who have escaped oppression, it is easy to see how the desire for a strong psychological wall between "us" and "them" was planted. In terms of betrayal, the mob at the gates is represented by the demonizer we examined in Chapter Two. Most recently, it has figured in President Bush's "axis of evil." As President Bush has stated, "You are either with us or against us." To put it mildly, this is a split of the strongest possible kind: the forces of "good" are fighting the forces of "evil."

(The mob at the gates myth was prominent at the Salt Lake City Winter Olympic Games of 2002. Literally hundreds of millions of dollars were spent preparing for *external* threats of terrorism. However, in the end, it was the *internal* problems of the International Olympic Committee that caused the crisis at the Winter Games. The point is that it is always easier to project one's defects onto outside forces than to face them as internal character flaws.)

The Rot at the Top

The rot at the top is the perennial myth that the common people are the repository of all goodness and instinctive common wisdom. If America has been betrayed, then it is by the powerful at the top—for instance, the hierarchy of the Catholic Church who, like European royalty, has been corrupted by unchecked power.

The Triumphant Individual

The triumphant individual is the quintessential American lone wolf, the solitary American hero who gets things done in his own quiet and determined way, who marches to his own drum, unconcerned for what the masses think. He has assumed various cloaks and guises during our history. At one time he has been a Charles Lindbergh, at another, a John Wayne, or a Clint Eastwood.

The Benevolent Society

The benevolent society is America itself, the perennial champion of the underdog, the provider to the tired, the poor, the hungry, the downtrodden of the planet yearning to be set free. It is an American myth that we can do no wrong because America is the fountainhead of all that is right. This myth is thus our self-idealization. As such, it is the counterpart to the demonizer—that is, the "axis of evil."

At this particular point in world history, of all of the American myths, the benevolent society is the one *not* shared by the rest of the world. Especially with the war in Iraq, the rest of the world does not share the belief that America is the preeminent "benevolent society." They question not only our basic purpose for being in Iraq but also our integrity. To many people in other countries, it is highly questionable that the United States is "goodness personified."

The Psychoanalytic Meanings

In psychoanalytic terms, the rot at the top myth is one of the primal fears of the young ego, the dread of the bad father, the evil kings from which we fled. Given that serfdom and servitude thrust even supposed mature adults back into a state of childhood dependence, America's infantile fears have an all-too-real basis. As we have learned, the human animal is inclined to exaggerate such fears even in the best of childhoods. The exaggeration must, then, be extreme and intense when there is some basis for it. Thus, the mob at the gates is our unchecked projection of the evil originally done to us by kings onto American's enemies, real as well as imagined. Also, since no people are ever perfect, the mob at the gates is the unconscious projection of our internal defects, our acknowledged evil sides, onto others. The benevolent society is, of course, the good, nurturing, beneficent mother, while the triumphant individual is the young ego, unfettered by any past or sense of history, strutting brashly across the world's stage.

The fear of winding down is the fear of losing the energy associated with the forever youthful triumphant individual. Similarly, the fear of falling away is the companion fear of losing the virtues and graces associated with the benevolent society. The relationship between Wilkinson's remaining two fears and Reich's other two myths is a bit more complicated. The fear of being owned is the fear of being overwhelmed or ruled by either the mob at the gates and/or the rot at the top. The fear of falling apart is the fear of disintegrating, splitting or flying apart, literally dying from either the mob at the gates and/or the rot at the top.

With these ideas in mind, we are merely one concept away from being able to explain more fully the factors that were responsible for the crises in Enron, the Catholic Church, and other examples.

Freudian Defense Mechanisms Apply to Institutions as Well as to Individuals

Institutions make use of the same defense mechanisms as individuals in order to deny their vulnerabilities to major crises (see

Table 2-1). Most often, they use these mechanisms to justify why they do *not* need to engage in effective crisis management (CM). For instance, consider the first defense mechanism, denial. Denial is used to ignore an organization's vulnerability to crisis. Somehow or another, the organization is exempt (see Table 2-1) from a whole class of crises (see Table 3-1), if not from crises altogether.

Unlike denial, disavowal at least recognizes the threat of a major crisis, but it downplays its importance. Prior to 9/11, this mechanism was used in abundance. Very few organizations could even admit their susceptibility to a large systems accident or crisis of any kind.

Table 2-1 can be used to assess both the kinds of defense mechanisms that an organization or institution uses and the extent to which each mechanism is used. In effect, the mechanisms constitute an organization's or an institution's culture with regard to CM. For instance, an organization or institution that subscribes to a preponderance of the mechanisms in Table 2-1 almost ensures that it will not take CM seriously. As a result, the organization or institution will have increased dramatically the odds that it will experience a crisis.

A Deeper Understanding

The concepts of this and the previous chapters allow us, finally, to have a deeper understanding of how crises result from the actions and inactions of organizations and institutions. Interestingly, the forces that produce crises across organizations as diverse as Enron/Andersen, the Catholic Church, and government agencies are essentially the same as those that were responsible for 9/11. These various forces are shown in Table 8-1. They help to explain the forces that led to the outrageous behavior in Enron (financial shenanigans), and The Catholic Church (covering up criminal behavior).

A Sense of Entitlement

A number of the factors shown in Table 8-1 combined to make Enron/Andersen, the Catholic Church, and other short-sighted institutions feel that not only their mission but also the people and the rules by which they operate were special. That is, the organizations or institutions had a special nature and mission. This allowed them to be exempt from the rules of ordinary society. Even worse, the organizations and institution were entitled to break the rules. In addition, they forged new rules. In the case of Enron, employees were fed the line, almost like the initiates of a cult, that they were forging a new and exciting venture. They were not only rewriting the rules of the energy business but reinventing it, if not reinventing business in general. In addition, employees were subject to harsh standards and evaluations. Not only were the requirements severe for entry into the organization, but the tests for remaining in them were equally severe.

In the case of Enron, there was the infamous "rank and yank" performance evaluation system. Members were routinely ranked and placed in one of five categories. Those in the bottom fifth were removed every couple of months, no matter how competent they were. Over time, the rankings had the effect of being both political and arbitrary: managers were trying to distinguish between people who were already performing at an extraordinarily high level. The ranking system promoted the development of a harsh, ruthless culture.

At Enron, a person was rewarded for contributing to the *special* mission of the organization. While reinventing the energy business may be too lofty and abstract to consider here, the real

Table 8-1. Major forces/factors leading to organizational and societal crises.

Forces/Factors	Subfactors
Special Nature of the Mission/ Organization	Spiritual monarchy Idealization Chosen Called Grandiosity New Reinvent the industry The best and the brightest Cognitive IQ matters more than Emotional or Ethical IQ Authoritarian Secrecy Compartmentalization Rigid hierarchy Strict obedience
Special Rules, Culture, Reward	Above the laws Superior Warranted to break the rules The normal rules don't apply One is authorized and entitled to break the rules One is exempt from the normal rules of society One is mandated to reinvent the rules
Sense of Worthiness/Self	
Collusion	Breakdown in regulatory agencies

(continues)

Table 8-1. (Continued).

Forces/Factors	Subfactors
	Underfunding Failure to do their job Emasculated Overly bureaucratized Simultaneously too rigid walls and not separable/rigid enough
Culture/Values	Brutal Severe Contempt Arrogant Ruthless Loyalty to the institution valued above all else Loyalty to superiors more important than to those served Addictive Disdainful Creative accounting
Reward Systems	Brutal Severe Rank and yank Fear Ruthless

mission was much more concrete: complete deals at all costs. The rules of this game were clearly known.

In every major crisis we have experienced over the past eighteen months, the Freudian mechanisms of idealization, grandiosity, compartmentalization, and projection were operating at high levels. Those on the inside who played by the rules were the "good guys," while those who were opposed to the mission of the organization were the "bad guys." The process of splitting was prominent (see Chapter Two).

All of the organizations and institutions placed high value on loyalty. Service to the organization or institution became paramount, not service to the company's real customers. The organizations were also governed by strict lines of authority. This in turn promoted secrecy. Little wonder that these organizations and institutions encouraged their employees to engage in coverups and blame external factors for their problems. The end result was that an individual's worth was measured in terms of how well he or she performed with regard to the system's evaluations.

Time and again, the major factor was the extreme sense of entitlement that executives felt. At the same time, because the executives were insulated and isolated from the outside world, they had little understanding of how they would be perceived by others. This is where the myth of the rot at the top becomes evident. By taking care of themselves, in effect by making themselves the ultimate clients, they embodied the rot at the top myth.

The suspicions of the public were exacerbated by collusion from regulatory agencies. Either through their emasculation—for instance, the reduction in funding—or staffing by previous members of the industries they were supposed to regulate, these overseers failed to exercise their responsibilities. This point is extremely critical: rarely is a crisis caused by a single factor. Collusion is almost always a fundamental part of every crisis and every betrayal. Thus, betrayal does not arise from a single individual, organization, or institution. All of these forces come together to produce organizations and institutions that are not only ripe for crises but almost guaranteed to have them. They are prone to commit massive acts of betrayal.

Splitting is a major factor in every case. There has been a significant split between the thinking, on the one hand, and the feelings or the emotions of the organization on the other hand. At the same time, there is the prevailing feeling that organizations are *invulnerable* to crises, hence they do not need to prepare for them. Each of these example organizations and institutions not only took on the role of the benevolent society, but believed deeply that it was the benevolent society.

The proof of the pudding—that is, the power of the fears and the myths discussed in this chapter—is that these fears and myths not only apply to U.S. society but also to organizations and institutions. For instance, the fear of winding down is a common theme in various accounts of the demise of Enron. At Enron, human energy was valued much more than the physical energy locked up in oil and gas.

It is never a single myth or fear that is involved in the demise of an organization or institution. And it is important to understand that these fears and the myths are not entirely bad. Each has a positive as well as a negative side. The problem of managing is that of controlling the good sides without incurring the dark sides of these fears. I am not, therefore, calling for an "energyless" individual, organization, institution, or society. Such a situation would stifle innovation. Instead, the central job of management is the responsible control of fears and myths.

The Transformation of Myths

Myths are never static. Old myths are constantly transformed and new myths are constantly born. Take, for instance, the fear of falling apart. There is no question that this fear still operates and always will. In fact, it is at the heart of normal accidents. However, from the standpoint of 9/11, a new fear has come into being, which I call the fear of being blown apart. This is the fear that underlies abnormal accidents.

Although he didn't put it into the same words, in his book *Normal Accidents*, Charles Perrow has given an exceedingly important analysis of the fear of falling apart.[3] To recall from Chapter One, Perrow argued that, because of the complexity of modern technologies, the potential for constant disaster is built into their everyday operations.[4] Consider a chemical plant. The number of connections between the pipes, the valves that control the flow of materials, and the processes involved are so complex that no human being can predict fully what reactions can take place. Because of this complexity and because humans are not up to the task of managing these technologies, the potential for failure is built into the system. Thus, the fear of falling apart is all too real.

In contrast, the crises of 9/11, Enron/Andersen, and the Catholic Church are examples of abnormal accidents. These were not due to acts of omission, but rather to acts of commission (see Table 1-1). Human-caused crises have clearly entered a new phase. It is one thing for catastrophes to occur as the result of improper human actions or inactions. It is quite another for them to occur as the result of deliberate, evil intentions.[5] We have moved from a world made unsafe by the complexities of the enormous systems we have constructed to a world that has been intentionally made unsafe by "evil characters." Thus, a fundamental shift has occurred in the seven basic assumptions we have been examining (see Table 8-2). The shift is one from a world made unsafe unintentionally to a world made unsafe intentionally. This same shift applies to all of the fundamental assumptions that are behind every act of betrayal. Notice carefully

Table 8-2. Basic assumptions that result from the shift to abnormal accidents.
1. The world has been made unsafe by evil characters external to us.
2. The world can be seen as a struggle between the good and just versus the bad and evil.
3. The world has been rendered unstable and unpredictable.
4. Evil appears to be unlimited; nonetheless, it can be contained and rooted out by the forces of good.
5. America is inherently good.
6. America is the embodiment of all that is good; we are not at fault for the evil that is to be found in today's world.
7. There was no way that we could have known that we were about to be attacked by evil.

that I am *not* saying that the assumptions in Table 8-2 are true. Instead, they are what too many Americans would like to believe is true.

Four Additional Myths

In conjunction with the fears and myths that we have examined thus far, four additional ones apply to U.S. society:

1. Exceptionalism
2. Particularism
3. Entitlement
4. Isolationism

As one of the opening quotations to this chapter testifies, exceptionalism is rooted deeply in the American experience. It is the belief that America is fundamentally exempt from the laws of history. America was founded to break free from the laws of history. It was literally the "grand experiment." In journeying to America, the Founding Fathers had the opportunity to create society anew, freed from the forces of history.

Particularism is the notion that America has been anointed and singled out by God for special attention, care, and protection. America has God's special blessing. In this sense, God "looks over and cares for America." As John Horgan puts it in his book *Rational Mysticism*:

> The essence of the doctrine is that God plays favorites. All these schemes ask us to believe in some sort of supernatural moral accountant who, like Santa Claus, keeps tabs on our naughtiness and niceness in order to determine our fate in the afterlife. As William James commented: "Any God who, on the one hand, can care to keep a pedantically minute account of individual shortcomings, and on the other hand can feel such partiality, and load particular creatures with such specific marks of favor, is too small-minded a God for our favor."[6]

A direct result of the first two myths is the notion of entitlement. If America is exceptional, and if it has been singled out by God for special attention, then it is entitled uniquely to rule the entire world. This particular notion does much to explain President Bush's belief that the United States has the inherent moral right to act unilaterally whenever it chooses to do so, independently of the rest of the world.

Isolationism is an expression of the tenet that the United States is somehow shielded from the rest of the world. In the extreme, it is the notion that the outside world doesn't matter at all or is of little importance and consequence. For most of its history, the United States has in fact been so isolated geographically from the rest of the world that, for all practical purposes, other countries didn't matter.

Concluding Remarks

Recent crises, but 9/11 in particular, have revealed the serious inadequacy of the myths that we have discussed to serve the American people. In effect, these myths are grand assumptions masquerading as myths about the nature of the world. The 9/11 attack was terrible not only because of the horrible physical destruction that it wrought, but because it demolished some of our most sacred assumptions about the nature of America and the world. The destruction of these assumptions has exacted a terrible blow on the American psyche. Worse still, there is no prospect for replacing them with others that are better suited for a complex world.

Notes

1. Robert Reich, *Tales of a New America* (New York: Times Books, 1987).
2. Rupert Wilkinson, *The Pursuit of American Character* (New York: Harper and Row, 1988).
3. Charles Perrow, *Normal Accidents: Living with High Risk Technologies* (New York: Basic Books, 1984).
4. Ibid.
5. The timeline of crises in Figure 1-1 must be taken with a strong word of caution. While I believe that the figure, and especially the implications that I have derived from it, are not artifacts, the determination of what is and what is not a "major crisis" is not without considerable argument. Indeed, the definition of what a "crisis" is depends very strongly on the assumptions that one makes about a particular situation. For this reason, the definition of key terms

is an important topic in itself. See, for instance, Ian I. Mitroff and Harold A. Linstone, *The Unbounded Mind* (New York: Oxford University Press, 1993).

6. John Horgan, *Rational Mysticism: Dispatches from the Border Between Science and Spirituality* (New York: Houghton Mifflin, 2003), pp. 46–50.

CHAPTER NINE

Epilogue: A Tale of Two Companies

American Pharmaceuticals and Protodyne Laboratories (not their real names) are major players in the pharmaceutical industry. From the outside, they seem exactly alike. They have roughly the same levels of sales and numbers of employees. Both operate worldwide and have the same number of plants and facilities scattered around the globe. Both companies have suffered multiple crises, and these crises have ranged from product tampering to employee sabotage and sexual harassment. That's where the similarities end.

American Pharmaceuticals is a prime example of a proactive company; Protodyne is a prime example of a reactive company. The latest crisis facing both companies concerns two different drugs that the companies manufacture. Both treat the same debilitating disease, but with entirely different approaches. American produces a drug by the name of Proviz that is taken orally, while Protodyne produces a drug by the name of A33, which is taken through daily injections. Both drugs went through extensive testing before they were approved by the Federal Drug Administration, or FDA.

The current crisis had its origin in the fact that both drugs involve extraction of an enzyme from laboratory animals. Over the past two years, activists from a radical animal rights group have infiltrated the ranks of both companies. In an effort to discredit the companies, members of the animal rights group have engaged in serious and repeated acts of product tampering. The deaths of several consumers have been traced directly to the consumption of the altered drugs.

Crisis Champions: Backgrounds

Dianne Stahl and Frank Diamond are the crisis champions at American and Protodyne, respectively. Formally, their titles are senior Crisis Management executives. Both have roughly the same number of years of experience, levels of education, authority, responsibility, and so on. Day by day and minute by minute, they try to help their organizations avoid or cope better with crises.

Dianne and Frank are extreme opposites. Their personalities and operating styles are completely different. Most people are mixtures of Mary and Frank, and hence they fall somewhere in between them. In spite of this, Dianne and Frank are real. Extremes such as Dianne and Frank do exist.

Using the methods described in earlier chapters, Dianne has successfully sold crisis management (CM) to her top management; Frank has not. Dianne has learned all of the key lessons of CM described in this book; Frank has not. Dianne has learned how to present those lessons such that they do not threaten top management; Frank has not. Dianne has learned how to translate the lessons into words that her top executives easily understand and respect; Frank has not. As a result, Frank gets blamed whenever crises occur; Dianne does not.

Dianne learned early on that she had to get people talking about how they felt, especially if they had witnessed harm, serious injury, or worse, death of a fellow worker. She also learned that people were seriously affected if they learned of the deaths of consumers. If employees clammed up and did not talk about their feelings, they took substantially longer to return to work and they instigated a greater number of lawsuits against the organization. Thus, if the initial crisis weren't bad enough, then the aftereffects became additional crises that were just as bad. In those situations where Dianne realized that it was beyond her capability to cope with grief of fellow workers, she called in trauma experts and grieving counselors who offered immediate help. She even sought counseling for herself and took courses in psychology at her local community college so she could understand how to make better use of trauma experts, and also how to understand her own feelings. Over time, she became an informal crisis counselor.

In the beginning, Dianne did most of this behind-the-scenes work so that top management who had not had such training would not engage in denial or, even worse, use Dianne as a scapegoat for avoiding their own feelings. After she had collected enough data to show conclusively that utilizing grief and trauma counselors resulted in substantial cost savings and dramatically fewer lawsuits, Dianne was ready to make her case to top management. She showed that by bringing in trauma experts, on average employees were absent from work for a shorter time—only eight weeks as compared to forty weeks if they did not receive proper counseling as soon as possible.

Dianne showed also that being proactive—that is, preparing for crises far in advance—paid off: it was good business. In fact, being proactive paid all kinds of unforeseen dividends. It not only helped the organization recover sooner and better from a crisis, but it also resulted in substantial improvements in the conduct of day-to-day business. For example, the skills developed in coping with crises led to direct improvements in quality control. American had fewer recalls of faulty products. It had fewer disgruntled workers. Indeed, CM turned out to be a system-wide improvement program. No wonder American had a significantly longer expected life span.

In contrast, Frank tried a purely cognitive or intellectual approach to CM. Because he was unable to acknowledge his own feelings of vulnerability—feelings that all crises invariably raise—he was unable to help others deal with their emotions. In a word, he dismissed the feelings of others. He came across as uncaring and unfeeling. No one wanted to listen to him or even be with him, for that matter. Whereas Dianne used both feelings and rationality to sell CM, Frank used only rationality. Because of his need to be in control, he came across as "crazy and irrational," the very things he tried too hard not to be.

Frank knew how to calculate and measure risks. Dianne knew how to manage crises. She knew both the tools of the trade—for example, risk analysis—and how to sell CM to the top so that they would take it seriously. She knew that all the best tools and techniques were for naught if she was unable to get top management to feel comfortable with her and buy into the concept of CM.

Dianne was high on cognitive—that is, traditional IQ and emotional IQ; Frank was high only on cognitive IQ. Dianne was able to deploy her full self as a person. Dianne was integrated; Frank was fragmented. Dianne was successful in her professional and private lives. Frank was unsuccessful in both.

How American and Protodyne Handled the Current Crisis

Let us examine briefly how Dianne and Frank each responded to the current product tampering crisis by animal rights activists. At the very first suspicion of serious product tampering, Dianne convened a group of executives from across American's different departments, functions, and units. This included people from Quality Control, but also from Security, Finance, Legal, Strategic Planning, and Issues Management. American realized the depth of anger against its research and its potential for further loss of life, as well as a Public Relations disaster. The company decided to launch a new research program that would replace the enzyme extraction and to minimize the testing with laboratory animals. As a consequence, the company won widespread public support and emerged from the crisis stronger and better.

In sharp contrast, Frank viewed the crisis largely as a Quality Control and a Security issue. Thus, Protodyne did not make substantial efforts to change its products or laboratory testing methods. Its actions angered not only animal rights groups but public interest groups even more. The crisis deepened and spread further.

The Moral

The moral of this story is not that women necessarily make better crisis champions than men, or that women are inherently better suited for the job. That is not the right conclusion at all. For every "Dianne" or other woman who is a good crisis champion, there is one who is poor. And conversely, for every "Frank" or other man who is poor, there is one who is good. The differences are due to character and aptitude, not gender.

In many organizations there is a lone crisis champion—a middle manager or worker—who tries to do the right thing merely because it is the right thing to do. The champion wages a constant battle against bureaucratic indifference and red tape. He or she struggles daily to get top management to recognize the crises and do what is needed that will prepare the organization to survive that major crisis.

Champions are motivated not only by the desire to do the right thing but also to save the jobs of their fellow workers. They are motivated by the desire to spare their communities harm from the psychological and environmental damage wrought by major crises. Everyone needs to—and can—learn to become a crisis champion in his or her organization and, more important, in life.

APPENDIX A

Major Crises at a Glance

Crisis	Date	Description	Injuries/Deaths/Damage
Three Mile Island	March 28, 1979	Malfunction at a nuclear power plant near Middletown, PA caused the core of the reactor to overheat.	No injuries or deaths, but it was the most serious accident in U.S. commercial nuclear power plant operating history.
Tylenol poisonings	September 29 to October 1, 1982	Product tampering involving cyanide being inserted into Tylenol Extra Strength capsules.	7 people in the Chicago area died. No one has ever been charged in this case.
Bhopal Disaster	December 3, 1984	Industrial accident that killed thousands of people in the Indian city of Bhopal in Madhya Pradesh, following the accidental release of forty tons of *methyl isocyanate* (MIC) from a Union Carbide chemical plant located in the heart of the city.	The Bhopal accident killed more than 2,000 people outright and injured anywhere from 150,000 to 600,000 others, some 6,000 of whom would later die from their injuries.

Crisis	Date	Description	Injuries/Deaths/Damage
Space Shuttle *Challenger* Explosion	January 28,1986	Space Shuttle *Challenger* explodes on take-off from the NASA Kennedy Space Center in Florida. The cause is later determined to be failure of an "O" ring due to extremely cold weather conditions.	All 7 astronauts aboard the *Challenger* died.
Chernobyl Disaster	April 25–26, 1986	One of the world's worst nuclear power accidents. The Chernobyl nuclear power plant, located 80 miles north of Kiev in the former Soviet Union (now Ukraine), went out of control resulting in explosions and a fireball which blew off the reactor's heavy steel and concrete lid.	The Chernobyl accident killed more than 30 people immediately, and as a result of the high radiation levels in the surrounding 20-mile radius, 135,000 people had to be evacuated.
Mad Cow Disease	1986 to present	Mad cow disease, or its scientific name Bovine Spongiform Encephalopathy (BSE), is a fatal brain-wasting disease in cattle which was first identified in the United Kingdom (UK) in 1986. The disease can be passed from infected meat to humans, also causing brain damage and, eventually, death.	153 human cases reported worldwide; of these, approximately 100 people have died. Millions of cattle were slaughtered in an effort to eliminate the disease.

Pan Am Flight 103	December 21, 1988	Pan Am flight 103 was blown out of the sky over Lockerbie, Scotland. Two Libyan citizens were later convicted of masterminding the bombing.	Deaths: 259 people on the plane and 11 on the ground.
Exxon Valdez Oil Spill	March 24, 1989	The *Exxon Valdez*, an oil tanker, crashed into rocks in Prince William Sound, Alaska. Millions of gallons of oil contaminated the fragile ecosystem.	Animal Deaths: 3,000 sea otters, 250,000 sea birds, 300 harbor seals, 250 bald eagles, 22 orcas (killer whales), and billions of fish and small sea creatures. More than two billion dollars was spent on the clean up, which was not completed until 1992.
Chilean Grape Scare	April, 1989	Chilean grapes were banned in the U.S. due to a terrorist threat and the finding of traces of a little cyanide on two grapes.	None.
LAPD—Rodney King beating	March 3, 1991	After a high-speed car chase in the San Fernando Valley, Rodney King, who is black, was beaten by white LAPD officers, as a sergeant directed from nearby. King sustained approximately fifty-six baton strokes, was kicked in the head and body, and stunned with a Taser stun gun. Some of the beating was captured on an amateur photographer's videotape, which was eventually viewed around the world.	None immediately (see the L.A. Riots below).

Crisis	Date	Description	Injuries/Deaths/Damage
L.A. Riots	April 29–May 4, 1992	The April 29, 1992 state court acquittal of the four officers involved in the Rodney King beating led to rioting that lasted 6 days. Thousands of people participated in the riots, and the violence and looting spread to other parts of Los Angeles County. Federal troops and the California National Guard were called in; the officers were subsequently tried on federal criminal civil rights charges. Sergeant Koon and Officer Powell were convicted of violating Rodney King's civil rights and sentenced to thirty months' imprisonment.	54 people were killed, 2,383 injured (221 critically), and 13,212 arrested. Property damage was estimated at more than $700 million for the county.
World Trade Center Bombing	February 26, 1993	A bomb exploded in a basement garage of the World Trade Center. In 1995, militant Islamist Sheik Omar Abdel Rahman and 9 others were convicted of conspiracy charges, and in 1998, Ramzi Yousef, believed to have been the mastermind, was convicted of the bombing. Al-Qaeda involvement is suspected.	6 deaths and 1,040 injuries.

Waco, Texas Standoff	February 28 to April 19, 1993	Agents of the Bureau of Alcohol, Tobacco, and Firearms raided the Branch Davidian compound to serve arrest and search warrants as part of an investigation into illegal possession of firearms and explosives there. Gunfire erupted and a 51-day siege ensued which culminated on April 19, 1993.	Deaths of 4 ATF agents, and injuries to 16, on February 28th; the resulting fire in the compound at the end of the siege on April 19th killed 80 Branch Davidians, including 22 children.
Syringes in cans of Pepsi	June 10–17, 1993	Two reports in the Seattle-Tacoma area of Washington state that consumers found syringes in cans of Diet Pepsi led to a regional FDA warning; within 24 hours, reports of syringes in Diet Pepsi cans came in from disparate locations, resulting in widespread media coverage. With no reasonable explanation from a manufacturing standpoint, the FDA recommended a course of no recall.	No injuries were reported; Pepsi incurred $25 million in lost sales revenue.
Somalia	October 3–4, 1993	Battle of Mogadishu in Somalia: A deadly shootout developed into the largest firefight since the Vietnam War after two Black Hawk helicopters were shot down during a mission to capture two lieutenants of the Somalian warlord General Mohamed Farrah Aidid.	The battle ended with the eventual deaths of 18 of America's most elite soldiers, and the wounding of 75 others. Estimates of Somali deaths varied between 500 and 1,500.

Crisis	Date	Description	Injuries/Deaths/Damage
Texaco Racism Scandal	August, 1994 to November, 1996	A senior personnel manager in Texaco's finance department taped an August 1994 meeting at which he and three other executives disparaged black workers and discussed hiding and destroying documents that were vital to a pending discrimination case. This tape set off a racial scandal at Texaco.	Texaco settled the case for an estimated $176 million in cash and other considerations—the largest such settlement on record.
Orange County Bankruptcy	December 6, 1994	Orange County, California became the largest municipality in U.S. history to declare bankruptcy after the county treasurer lost $1.7 billion of taxpayer money through investments in risky Wall Street securities.	No deaths or injuries.
Kobe Earthquake	January 17, 1995	Earthquake measuring 7.2 on the Richter scale struck Kobe, Japan.	5,100 deaths; 300,000 people left homeless. The cost to restore the basic infrastructure of the city was about $150 billion dollars.
Barron's Crisis	1995	Financial crisis at Barron's Bank brought about by risky Japanese investments which failed after the Kobe earthquake.	No deaths or injuries.

Tokyo Subway Attacks	March 20, 1995	Act of domestic terrorism perpetrated by members of AUM Shinrikyo. In five coordinated attacks, AUM members released sarin gas on several lines of the Tokyo Subway. This was the most serious terrorist attack in Japan's modern history.	12 deaths and 6,000 injuries.
Oklahoma City Bombing	April 19, 1995	Domestic terrorist attack on the Alfred P. Murrah Federal Building in Oklahoma City, OK. The attack was in retaliation for the deaths in 1993 at the Branch Davidian compound in Waco, Texas.	168 people, including 19 children, died in the explosion. Timothy McVeigh was later convicted of the bombing and executed by the Federal government.
Crash of ValuJet Flight 592	May 11, 1996	Airplane disaster aboard a Miami-to-Atlanta flight. The plane crashed into the Florida Everglades shortly after takeoff; it was later determined that the crash was due to a cargo fire caused by oxygen canisters which were mistakenly labeled and improperly packed in the cargo hold.	All 110 people aboard the plane perished. As a result of the crisis, ValuJet was forced into bankruptcy. It was later reorganized as a new low-cost airline.

Crisis	Date	Description	Injuries/Deaths/Damage
TWA Flight 800	July 17, 1996	TWA Flight 800, a Boeing 747 bound for Paris, exploded shortly after takeoff from New York's Long Island. The FAA ruled that the explosion was caused by a spark of unknown origin in the fuel tank; there was much speculation that the plane was brought down by a shoulder-fired missile after 270 people provided the FBI with accounts of an unknown object which streaked up from the horizon and arced toward TWA Flight 800 in the seconds before it exploded.	All 230 people on board the plane perished.
US Army Sexual Harassment Scandal	April to September, 1996	Sexual harassment scandal involving 12 officers at the U.S. Army's Aberdeen Proving Grounds near Baltimore, MD. The officers were accused of sexual abuses against females under their command, which included charges of rape, sodomy, and assault.	An Army hotline set up in November, 1996 to field complaints of sexual harassment was flooded with about 5,000 calls, resulting in 325 investigations of misconduct at army installations around the world.

Nazi Gold	September, 1996	Discovery of paper trail linking gold in Switzerland to that which was looted by the Nazis between 1939 and 1945. The gold included bullion bars, trinkets from jeweler's shops, and gold from the teeth of those who died in the death-camps. Calls issued to make restitution to the Holocaust survivors and/or their descendants.	The gold was worth around $400 million when it was looted ($3.9 billion in today's values). About ¾ of the money was kept in the Swiss National Bank and the remainder went to accounts in other countries.
LAPD Ramparts Scandal	May, 1998 to November, 2000	A special task force was set up to investigate misconduct by more than 70 officers at LAPD's Rampart Station Anti-Gang unit. The officers were investigated for either committing crimes (routinely engaging in illegal shootings, beatings, perjury, false arrests, witness intimidation, and other misconduct) or knowing about them and helping to cover them up.	L.A. City Attorney's office estimated that total Rampart-related settlement costs would total $125 million; the LAPD's elite anti-gang unit CRASH was disbanded and court-ordered injunctions against gang members were suspended.
Attacks on U.S. Embassies	August 7, 1998	Near simultaneous terrorist attacks on the U.S. Embassies in Nairobi, Kenya, and Dar es Salaam, Tanzania. 17 individuals, including Osama Bin Laden, are charged with the crimes.	*Kenya*: 12 American diplomats, 34 Kenyan U.S. Embassy employees, and 167 citizens of Nairobi near the embassy at the time were killed, making a total of 213 dead. *Tanzania*: 10 deaths and 70 injuries.

Crisis	Date	Description	Injuries/Deaths/Damage
Clinton-Lewinsky Affair	August, 1998	President Clinton, after 9 months of near silence, admitted that he did have an affair with ex-White House intern Monica Lewinsky. The President was later impeached by the Senate, but was acquitted on the charges of perjury before the grand jury and obstruction of justice.	N/A
Turkey Earthquake	August 17, 1999	An earthquake measuring between 7.4 and 7.9 on the Richter Scale occurs near Izmit, an industrial city about 55 miles east of Istanbul on the Sea of Marmara. At least 300 aftershocks followed in the first 48 hours.	More than 14,000 dead and 200,000 left homeless. Contractors convicted of constructing shoddy buildings which were responsible for the deaths and injuries.
Ford-Firestone Tire Crisis	May to August, 2000	Firestone tire recall is the most deadly auto safety crisis in American history. Most of the deaths occurred in accidents involving the Ford Explorer, which tends to rollover when one of the tires blows out and/or the tread separates.	More than 200 deaths and 800 injuries were linked to defective Firestone tires. The recall cost Ford $500 million in lost production. Both companies were the targets of a large number of lawsuits that likely will take years—and millions, if not billions—to settle.

California Energy Crisis	May, 2000 to May, 2001	By the early 1990s, electricity rates in California were on average 50% higher than the rest of the U.S. The three major privately held utility companies (Southern California Edison, Pacific Gas & Electric, and San Diego Gas & Electric) spent $4.3 million on lobbyists and $1 million on political campaigns in their efforts to encourage deregulation. In 1995, the state legislature unanimously passed a bill to open the industry to competition, but consumers ended up paying almost twice the rate they did before deregulation, and suffering rolling blackouts.	Nearly 60 companies were allegedly involved in a price fixing scam that precipitated California's 2000–2001 energy crisis. A coalition including the CPUC and the state's attorney general demanded $7.5 billion in consumer refunds and almost $9 billion to cover the cost of emergency energy purchases.
Concorde Crash	July 25, 2000	Concorde jet bound for New York crashed shortly after taking off from the Paris airport. It was eventually determined that the plane hit a metal strip on the runway, causing debris to burst under-wing fuel tanks and start the fire that brought the plane down.	Deaths: 109 people on the plane, and 4 on the ground.
U.S.S. Cole Attack	October 12, 2000	Terrorist bomb attack against the *USS Cole* while it refueled in the Yemeni port of Aden.	17 sailors killed and 39 injured.

Crisis	Date	Description	Injuries/Deaths/Damage
9/11	September 11, 2001	Terrorist attacks carried out against the World Trade Center in New York and the Pentagon in Washington, D.C. Both buildings were struck by commercial airliners which had been highjacked by Al Qaeda terrorists. A third airplane crashed into a field in Pennsylvania.	*Death toll in the attacks*: 2749 in the World Trade Center 189 in the Pentagon 44 in the plane crash near Shanksville, PA ——— Total deaths: 2982
Anthrax Attacks	September–October, 2001	Bioterrorist attacks involving the mailing of anthrax spores through the U.S. Post Office. Several attacks at various locations around the country resulted in numerous exposures, infections, and fatalities. Thousands were tested and 10,000 people in the United States took a two-month course of antibiotics after possible exposure.	19 infections and 5 fatalities.

Enron/ Andersen	December, 2001	Houston-based Enron went bankrupt in December 2001 amid revelations of hidden debt, inflated profits, and accounting tricks. Enron's auditor (Arthur Andersen) was convicted of obstruction of justice, fined the maximum amount allowable by law ($500,000), and was given a five-year probation.	The bankruptcy is one of the most expensive in history, generating more than $665 million in fees for lawyers, accountants, consultants, and examiners (according to the Texas Attorney General's Office). The bankruptcy plan proposes to pay most creditors about one-fifth of the nearly $70 billion they are owed in cash and stock.
Martha Stewart Insider Trading Scandal	December 27, 2001	Martha Stewart was found guilty of conspiracy, obstruction, and two counts of lying to investigators for covering up the circumstances surrounding her Dec. 27, 2001 stock trade of biotech company ImClone. Stewart is a good friend of ImClone's former CEO, and she sold $228,000 worth of ImClone stock the day before the Food and Drug Administration rejected the company's promising new cancer drug.	Martha Stewart was sentenced to six months in a minimum-security prison.

Crisis	Date	Description	Injuries/Deaths/Damage
Pedophilia Crisis in the Catholic Church	2002	A national study of Catholic Church records found that about 4% of U.S. priests ministering from 1950 to 2002 were accused of sex abuse with a minor. The Church hierarchy is also accused of systematically covering up the problem: roughly two-thirds of top U.S. Catholic leaders have allowed priests accused of sexual abuse to keep working.	4,392 clergymen—almost all priests—were accused of abusing 10,667 people, with 75% of the incidents taking place between 1960 and 1984. Sex-abuse related costs totaled $573 million as of 2002, but the overall dollar figure is much higher than reported because 14% of the dioceses and religious communities did not provide financial data and the total did not include settlements made after 2002, such as the $85 million agreed to by the Boston Archdiocese.
WorldCom	June 25, 2002	WorldCom, the second largest long distance provider in the United States, announced it filed bankruptcy. As a result of an internal audit, $4 billion in expenses had been improperly categorized as capital expenditures rather than as operating expenses. The effect was to overstate cash flow and profitability. Arthur Andersen was WorldCom's accounting firm.	17,000 WorldCom employees were laid off.

SARS	November 2002 to July, 2003	Severe acute respiratory syndrome (SARS) is a viral respiratory illness caused by a coronavirus. SARS was first reported in Asia in February 2003. Over the next few months, the illness spread to more than two dozen countries in North America, South America, Europe, and Asia before the SARS global outbreak of 2003 was contained.	8,098 people worldwide became sick with SARS during the 2003 outbreak. Of these, 774 died.
Columbia Disaster	February 1, 2003	The Space Shuttle *Columbia* breaks apart over Western Texas on re-entry to the earth's atmosphere. The accident was triggered by the incredible heat generated from atmospheric friction entering the interior of the left wing, causing it to melt from within until it failed and broke free. When this occurred the shuttle spun out of control and disintegrated.	All 7 astronauts aboard the shuttle died in the accident.

Crisis	Date	Description	Injuries/Deaths/Damage
East Coast Power Outages	August 14–15, 2003	A massive power blackout which spread through the northeastern United States and southern Canada. It was the biggest power outage in U.S. history, and within three minutes, 21 power plants in the United States had shut down. At its peak, the outage reportedly affected more than 50 million people.	Three deaths were tied to the outage, and it cost New York City alone over a half-billion dollars in lost revenue.
New York Stock Exchange Crisis	August–September, 2003	Problems with the corporate governance structure of the NYSE came to light when it was disclosed that Richard Grasso, NYSE president and chief operating officer, was going to receive a retirement package totaling $187.5 million. Many of the NYSE traders were angered that Grasso had extracted such a big pay package at the same time that their own paychecks were shrinking. The Securities and Exchange Commission began an inquiry and, after much pressure, Grasso resigned on September 17, 2003.	N/A

Mutual Funds	October–November, 2003	Putnam, the fifth biggest mutual fund in the U.S., was charged with improper trading by the Securities and Exchange Commission (SEC) and Massachusetts financial regulators. The SEC was criticized for slackness in overseeing the $7 trillion mutual funds industry, resulting in calls for a crackdown on some industry practices. Of specific concern are "market timing" practices which involve profiting from short-term trading in mutual fund shares, but can damage the value of the fund for long-term investors.	N/A
U.S. Mad Cow Scare	December, 2003	Mad cow disease was discovered in a cow in Washington state, prompting federal officials to recall more than 10,000 pounds of meat. The meat had been shipped to 8 states and Guam. The diseased cow was determined to have originally come to the U.S. from Canada. A number of nations banned U.S. beef imports once the case was announced.	N/A

APPENDIX B

A Brief Primer on Crisis Management

Crisis management (CM) is systemic. It is the process of thinking about a wide range of potential crises and how they can happen to any business. In addition, it is anticipating the broad range of systems whose failure can cause crises. Finally, it is about planning for the actions of a wide variety of stakeholders that affect, and in turn are affected by, major crises.

Crisis management is not risk management (RM), business continuity planning (BCP), or crisis communications (CC). While RM, BCP, and CC are important, they are only parts of the total CM process.

The Four Factors and the Three Phases

Figure B-1 shows that there are four major factors, or variables, involved in CM. Figure B-1 also shows that CM involves three major phases: before, during, and after a crisis. The "before" phase is concerned with exposing the weaknesses in an organization that can lead to a potential crisis. It involves building the actual capabilities needed to manage crises before they occur.

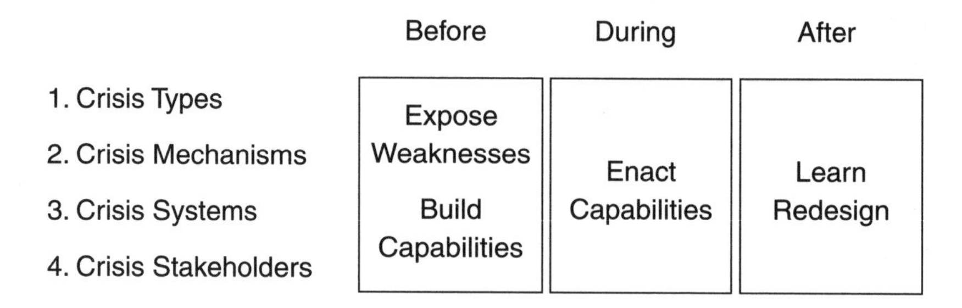

Figure B-1. The four factors of CM.

As Chapter Two demonstrates, crises generally unleash so many powerful emotions that it is extremely difficult, if not dangerous, to react to them without prior training and preparation. The "before" phase builds these actual capabilities. The "during" phase is the actual crisis. This phase is concerned ideally with enacting the capabilities that have been developed before the crisis. The "after" phase is for learning lessons from the crisis, redesigning the organization's crisis capabilities, and instituting the systems necessary to perform better when the next crisis occurs.

The Types of Crises That Can Occur

Figure B-2 and Table B-1 (which appeared in Chapter 3 as Table 3-1) show that crises fall into a limited number of distinct categories or types. This means that a company does not have to prepare for every conceivable kind of crisis—a virtual impossibility. Instead, the best organizations—those that we labeled as proactive in Chapter One—find it sufficient to prepare for *at least one* crisis in each of the categories.

Since no crisis ever occurs exactly as one has planned for it, it is crucial to learn how to think about the unthinkable and roll with the punches. Thus, it does not matter, for instance, whether

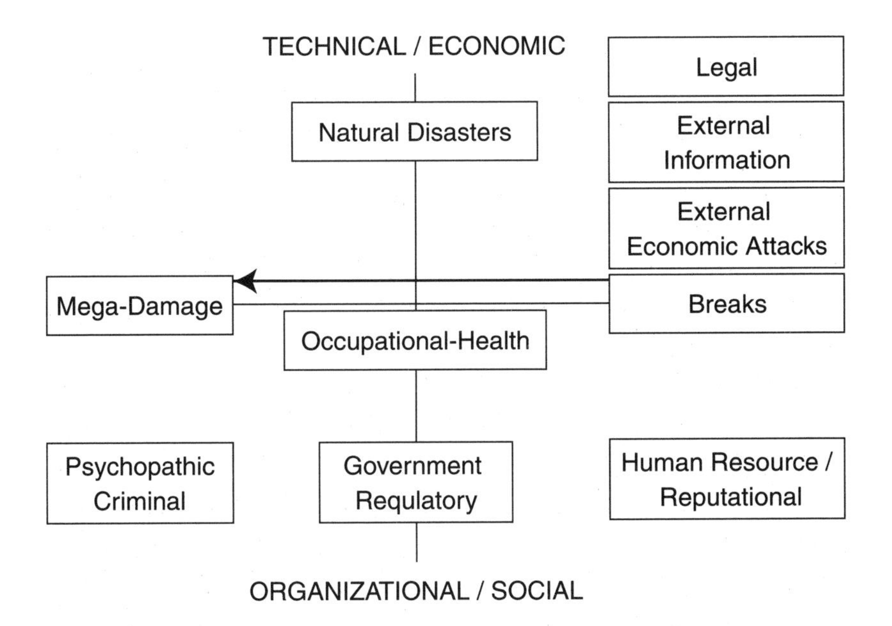

Figure B-2. Crisis types.

an organization has prepared for all kinds of "external information" attacks (see Table B-1) that can occur. All that matters is that the organization has prepared for at least one crisis in this category. Indeed, as indicated in Chapter One, organizations that are prepared for at least one crisis in each of the categories respond better, act sooner, and recover faster than those organizations that have not.

Table B-1 gives a fuller description of each of the subtypes of crises in the general categories. Figure B-2 shows a thick arrow going from the category "Breaks" to the box "Mega-Damage." "Breaks" stands for the type of unintended breakdown of technology that can cause mega-environmental damage such as a Chernobyl or *Exxon Valdez.*

The critical point about Figure B-2 is that since no crisis ever

Table B-1. Major types of crises.

Economic	Informational	Physical (Loss of key plants and facilities and products)	Human Resource
Labor strikes	Loss of proprietary and confidential information	Loss of key equipment, plants, and material supplies	Loss of key executives
Labor unrest	False information	Breakdowns of key equipment, plants, etc.	Loss of key personnel
Labor shortage	Tampering with computer records	Loss of key facilities	Rise in absenteeism
Major decline in stock price and fluctuations	Loss of key computer information with regard to customers, suppliers, etc.	Major plant disruptions	Rise in vandalism and accidents
Market crash	Y2K	Explosions	Workplace violence
Decline in major earnings		Faulty or poor product design	Lack of succession plans
Hostile takeovers		Product failures	Corruption
		Poor quality control	

Reputational	Psychopathic Acts	Natural Disasters
Slander	Product tampering	Earthquakes
Gossip	Kidnapping	Fires
Sick jokes	Hostage taking	Floods
Rumors	Terrorism	Typhoons
Damage to corporate reputation	Workplace violence	Hurricanes
Tampering with corporate logos	Criminal/ terrorist/ psychopathic acts	Mudslides
False rumors		

happens in isolation, a crisis in *any* of the boxes in Figure B-2 can be *both* the cause and the effect of *any* other crisis. This means that an organization must not prepare crisis plans in isolation. Instead, an organization must think and prepare systemically.

Crisis Mechanisms

Figure B-3 shows the variables that constitute the second factor in Figure B-1. The figure indicates that, in general, all crises are preceded by early warning signals. Thus, if an organization has a signal-detection capability, then it may be able to head off a major crisis—the best possible form of CM. The second box of Figure B-3 shows that signal detection should be coupled with active probes for defects or latent crises within an organization.

The box "Damage Containment" shows that even with the best preparations and probing, in today's world a crisis is virtually guaranteed to occur. Thus, "damage containment" means exactly what it says. Its purpose is to keep a crisis—for instance, fires, oil spills, nasty rumors—from spreading, contaminating, and infecting the rest of the organization.

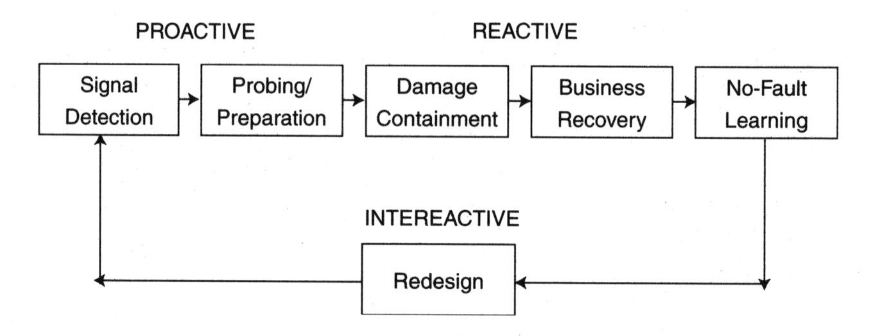

Figure B-3. Crisis mechanisms.

The next box, "Business Recovery," is primarily where business continuity planning (BCP) takes place. Thus, in this sense, BCP is a subset of CM, although, to be fair, many of those who practice BCP urge companies to use a much broader perspective—for instance, to make signal detection an integral part of BCP.

Finally, no-fault learning is an integral part of CM as well. That is, except in cases of criminal culpability and liability, organizations are strongly advised not to blame a crisis on particular individuals (see Chapter Two), but instead to learn the lessons that every crisis has to teach and to use that acquired knowledge to redesign an organization with improved crisis performance.

Crisis Systems

Figure B-4 shows that all crises are the result of breakdowns within complex systems. Indeed, these systems are synonymous with complex organizations. Figure B-4 indicates that every organization has a set of technologies it needs to conduct its business. In today's world, this includes at least information technologies. Unless they are managed properly, these information technologies are often the source of major crises or can exacerbate them.

All organizations have a certain structure. The structure that is needed to manage a crisis is not necessarily the same structure that is in place to conduct everyday business. If too much time is lost in shifting from the operational structure to the crisis management structure, then the crisis will invariably become worse.

Another important variable is the human factor. All technologies are both designed and operated by humans, and if anything is characteristic of humans, and organizations, it is that they make errors. Indeed, one of the most prevalent sources of errors

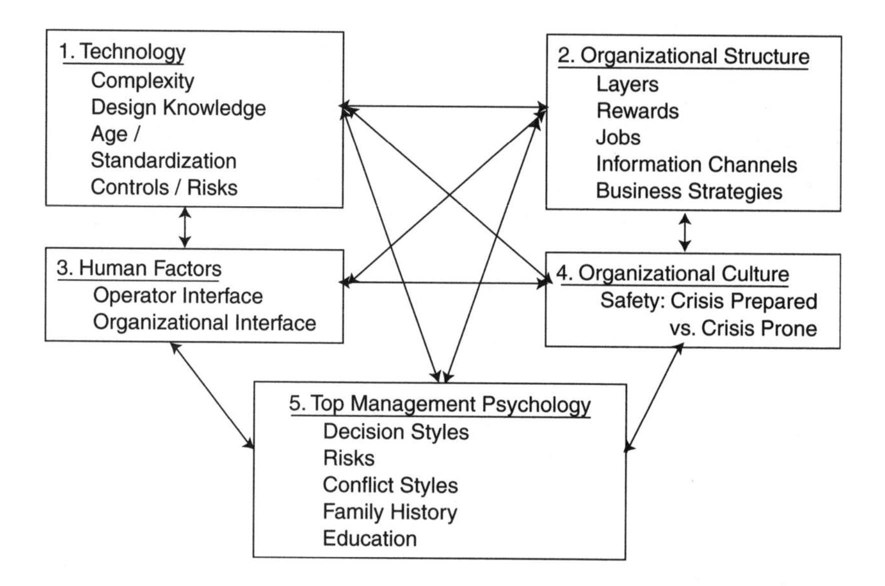

Figure B-4. Crisis systems.

is the misdesign of control panels—for instance, in nuclear reactors or hospital operating rooms.

Additionally, a major source of error is an organization's culture—specifically, how much it values safety and puts resources toward preserving it. Indeed, as we saw in Chapter One, there are immense differences between crisis-prepared or proactive organizations and crisis-prone or reactive organizations. Finally, the psychology of top management is a major factor in how much attention will be paid to CM.

Stakeholders and Their Influence

Stakeholders are all those parties, including organizations, that affect or are affected by major crises. In today's world, all organizations are impacted by innumerable stakeholders. Figure B-5

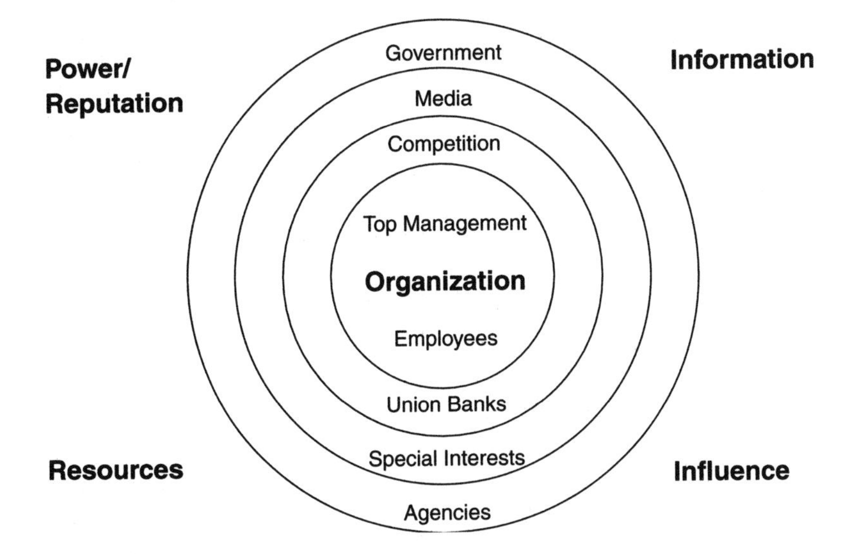

Figure B-5. Crisis stakeholders.

shows that stakeholders differ not only in their proximity to an organization but also in the major ways they can influence them. For instance, stakeholders differ in the amount of information they possess, the social and political influence they can bring to bear, the power or reputation that they have, and their resources.

An Ideal CM Program

Table B-2 shows the components of an ideal CM program. For instance, proactive organizations make CM a top corporate priority. In other words, CM is viewed as an integral part of corporate governance.

Point 2 in the table, a robust crisis portfolio, means that ideally the organization prepares for at least one crisis in each of the categories in Figure B-2 and Table B-1.

Table B-2. Components of an ideal CM program.
1. CM is a top corporate priority.
2. Robust crisis portfolio.
3. Constantly improving signal detection/probing/damage containment, etc.
4. Constantly audit systems: technology X culture.
5. Constantly audit/incorporate stakeholders into CM plans.
6. Pre-trauma CM training/simulations.
7. Integrate CM with Total Quality Management, Safety, Issues Management, Environmentalism, and Strategic Planning.

Concluding Remarks

Proactive crisis management has the following imperatives:

1. Anticipate and be prepared for a wide variety of crises.
2. Pick up and amplify the early warning signals that accompany all crises.
3. Institute damage-containment mechanisms early in a crisis in order to prevent it from spreading.
4. Form and train appropriate CM teams in order to have the necessary expertise to handle a wide variety of crises.
5. Continually audit the corporate culture for values that hinder effective CM.
6. Anticipate and include diverse stakeholders into the crisis plans and procedures.

Reactive organizations react primarily to "known" crises *after* they have occurred. Reactive CM also mainly uses the tools of RM.

	Risk Management	Business Continuity Planning	Crisis Communications	Crisis Management
Proactive?	Limited	Limited	Limited	Yes
Signals?	No	No	No	Yes
Damage Contain?	?	?	No	Yes
Org / Systems?	?	Yes	No	Yes
Low P / Hi C?*	No	No	No	Yes
Physical?	Yes	Yes	Yes	Yes
Psychological?	No	?	?	Yes
Spiritual?	No	No	No	Yes

*Low probability, high consequence.

Figure B-6. A comparison of RM, BCP, CC, and CM.

Finally, Figure B-6 identifies and contrasts proactive CM versus RM, BCP, and CC. Only proactive CM is systemic and therefore encompasses all the aspects of effective CM.

APPENDIX C

A Theory of Complex Problem-Formulation and Problem-Solving Inquiry Systems

In a long series of publications, Russ Ackoff, C. West Churchman, and I have explicated the nature of various inquiry systems. Inquiry systems are distinctively different archetypal systems for conducting inquiry. These have appeared time and again in the course of human history. The systems differ radically as to what they regard as knowledge—that is, what they define as knowledge and the conditions under which one can be said to have attained knowledge about a critical problem or issue.

One of the most important outcomes of the comparative study of inquiry systems is the recognition that some systems are inherently better suited for well-structured problems. In contrast, others are better suited for ill-structured problems. Unfortunately, it is beyond the purpose of this appendix to describe these systems in detail. Suffice it to say that those systems that are better suited for treating ill-structured problems regard the intense conflict between stakeholders as an important facilitator, and even a necessary precondition, for inquiry itself. They certainly do not regard conflict as an impediment to inquiry. Instead, they use the intense conflict between stakeholders regarding the basic nature and definition of a problem to expose different underlying assumptions regarding respective views of the world. In effect, these differing assumptions are fundamental parts of the "mess." They cannot be ignored or wished away. The upshot is that the ability to tolerate and manage conflict is an essential part of the CM process. In sum, inquiry systems differ radically with regard to the recognition of "mess management" as an area for inquiry and as an important component of that inquiry.

Systems Models of Science and CM

Instead of describing inquiry systems in a general way, I want to present two systems models or frameworks for understanding (1) science and (2) CM. The models reveal the complexity of both activities and, hence, why each is an ill-structured mess or, at the very least, has important aspects that are strongly ill-structured.

In 1974, Francisco Sagasti and I published a general systems model of scientific inquiry. We called it simply "the diamond model" (see Figure C-1.) Its purpose was to show where the major features of scientific inquiry lay in relation to one another, and how and why they were mutually dependent. The diamond model shows that scientific inquiry typically starts with the upper top box or activity—the "felt recognition or sensing" of a problem. I say "typically" because one of the purposes of the model is to show that an inquiry can start at any point. Also, there are a great number of directions, paths, or ways that one can proceed through the model.

In many ways, where problems come from is as mysterious

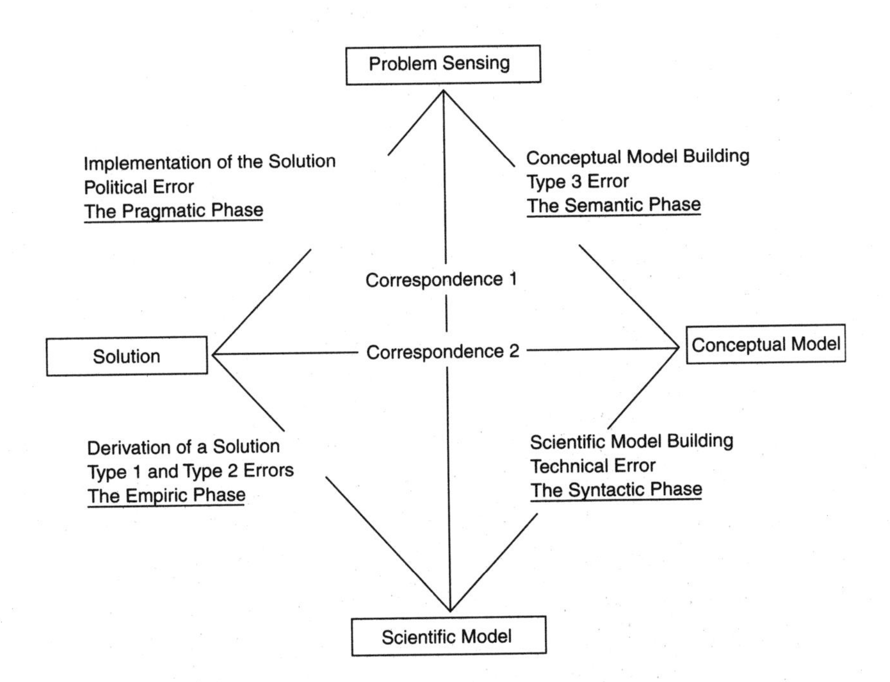

Figure C-1. The diamond model of scientific inquiry: *Transdisciplinary* systems thinking.

as the origin of the universe. We think we know the answers, but as soon as we try to justify our knowledge systematically, the argument becomes murky or, in the terms of this book, messy and ill-structured.

For the purpose of this appendix, problems are *"relatively" structured messes that have been extracted from highly unstructured messes for the purpose of managing better current and future messes.* Every aspect of this definition is, and is meant to be, tortuous and problematic. For instance, what do "extraction," "management," and "better" mean? "Extraction" is certainly a key activity because problems are not "given," but instead are "taken" from "reality." That is, problems do not drop preformed from the sky, or already structured. Instead, problems are the result of human activities of which extraction and shaping are merely two.

To be sure, many problems are "given" in the sense that they are merely extensions of previously predefined problems of one's discipline, field, profession, and so on. That is, one's discipline supplies the problems. However, even in such cases, the situation is not completely clear, for one has to explain how "extensions" are arrived at. Without a doubt, "problem sensing" is one of the more creative human activities. The most creative is certainly "problem invention," as in the cases of Freud, Gödel, and Einstein.

John Dewey regarded problem sensing as an inherently ethical activity, in the sense that many problems originated in moral outrage. For instance, many of our most important problems begin with moral outrages such as "How could they [the Catholic Church, Enron, the governor of the State of California, or the like] do or failed to have done such and such?" Certainly, many crises arise in moral outrage, and in this sense, they possess features that are undeniably ethical.

The important point is that problems are extracted from messes, and that the process of extraction is itself one of life's most important problems. Notice that in saying this—that is, uttering the immediately proceeding sentence—I am thereby being self-reflective, one of the hallmarks of philosophic thinking. I am turning the model or thinking about problems back on itself.

The upper diagonal line that proceeds from problem sensing, the felt existence or "fuzzy recognition" of a problem, to the existence of a conceptual model of the problem denotes the *process* of building a conceptual model or representation of the initial feeling or felt sense. It represents the *semantic* or the *problem formulation* phase of scientific problem solving because, at this point, we are concerned primarily with the broad meaning of a problem. We are dealing with the choice of an initial and even tentative discipline, disciplines, or languages in terms of which to represent the "basic meaning or definition" of the problem.

Notice carefully that, in terms of the diamond model, defining is part of the total process of inquiry. Defining is not a thing per se that exists apart from inquiry. Instead, defining is a tool that either enables or restrains the process of inquiry. As such, it cannot be ripped artificially from its moorings. Defining neither exists nor functions apart from the system of which it is a part. Thus, we cannot understand it in isolation. In contrast to the type I and the type II errors of statistics,[1] the error that pertains to this phase of the scientific problem-solving process is known as the type III error, or E3 for short. E3 is defined as "the error of solving the 'wrong' problem precisely." It is also defined as "the probability of solving the 'wrong' problem when one should have solved the 'right' problem."

Now, "right" and "wrong" are obviously relative. If we knew for sure that we were solving the wrong problem, then we would not be committing an E3. More important, the initial problem would already be well-structured so that there would be no need for problem formulation or problem structuring! Even in this case, there could still be enormous dispute as to whether we were indeed "solving the 'right' problem."

The point is that this phase of scientific problem solving is meant to call attention to the fact that the determination of an E3 can be made only if we produce at least two very different representations of a problem. Thus, the process of "rational" scientific problem solving calls for, at minimum, the use of those inquiry methods that are founded upon conflict—that is, sharp challenge of the different assumptions that stakeholders make about problems. This is merely one of the ways that scientific inquiry calls for other inquiry systems currently in conventional or widespread use.

Although there is always the possibility of revisiting for the purpose of revising one's initial conceptualization—the diamond model is not meant to imply that the process is linear and proceeds in only one way—the process of problem formulation terminates with the production of a conceptual model of the problem. The conceptual model lays out the main variables and the general features of the problem. It is not yet an exact scientific model of the problem, although often many features of the diamond model go on simultaneously such that they cannot easily be differentiated from one another. The diamond model exists, after all, to lay out the various features and processes inherent in scientific inquiry and not to imply that they are totally separate. Indeed, one of the basic definitions and properties of systems is that they are strongly inseparable.

The purpose of the next phase is to construct—using the tools of mathematics, flow charts, and the knowledge of physical, social, and historical processes—a precise representation, or "exact model," of the problem. This phase is known as the *syntactic phase of scientific problem solving.* It necessitates detailed knowledge of the rules for building exact models from word or conceptual models and the ability to execute the rules so as to produce a scientific model.

Science is replete with examples of outstanding models. One of the best is surely Einstein's transformation of his highly intuitive thought experiments and notions regarding space, time, mass, and gravity into complex mathematical equations. The first vertical line of correspondence between the initial felt sense of a problem and its "exact" scientific representation should not be interpreted as the correspondence between an "*objective,* external reality" and a "*subjective,* internal idea." This is wrong, plain wrong. Whatever "reality" is, it is as much a "representation" by and of our minds and culture as anything is. And surely, if human experience and perception mediate anything, it is the "felt sense or existence" of a problem.

This is not to deny the existence of external objects or crises. It is to deny that whatever "they are," they are not known and experienced independently of our minds and culture. In this sense, the common distinction between "objective" and "subjective" ought to be completely purged from common usage. It is a carryover from an earlier, primitive philosophy. It hinders knowledge and inquiry more than it helps. Modern philosophers have rejected the notion that our minds are blank tablets that do not participate actively in the experience of the world. John Dewey for one rejected this notion by referring to it dismissively as the "spectator theory of knowledge."

The next phase consists of deriving a solution to the scientific model or, more generally, testing a scientific hypothesis empirically. For this reason, it is the empiric phase of scientific problem solving. And, it also concerns the traditional type I and type II errors of statistics.

Notice carefully that the solution is not necessarily the solution to the initial problem, but it is the solution to the scientific model of the problem, which is in turn dependent on the conceptual model of the problem. Thus, the solution is at least twice removed from the initial problem. The point is once again how heavily the entire process relies on human experience and perception. Science is an intensely human enterprise through and through.

The so-called last phase—implementation—is the pragmatic phase of scientific problem solving. It is concerned with the social and political means of getting a solution accepted and adopted in a complex organization to remove the initial problem. Thus, implementation tests whether a problem can be removed or managed in practice, not merely in theory. Implementation also examines whether putting the solution into practice creates new problems or necessitates new formulations. Thus, the process is iterative.

Notice also that there is no requirement that the model be run in any particular direction or that it start with any particular point. Indeed, distinct forms of inquiry can be identified by the special paths through the model with which they are associated. The essential point is that scientific inquiry is a tightly coupled and highly interactive system. Its various parts neither exist nor function independently of one another.

Finally, notice that the process of defining anything is equivalent to the process of inquiry outlined in the diamond model. That is, the initial felt sense of a problem is equivalent to working or starting the definition of a problem. The definition of a problem is thus the outcome of inquiry, not the start.

We are now in a better position to give a sense of the differences between well-structured and ill-structured problems. Well-structured problems are problems for which a relatively few iterations of the diamond model are sufficient for the definition and the solution to converge. The implementation also tends to remove the initial problem. In other words, the mess generally lessens over time. In contrast, ill-structured problems misbehave over time. They generally get worse in the sense that the mess or the messes of which they are associated with grow, sometimes uncontrollably. This difference is often, but not always, the difference between disasters and crises. It is not always true that disasters are more well-structured and that crises are more ill-structured, because in today's complex world both are increasingly inseparable parts of messes.

A Diamond Model of CM

Figure C-2 is a parallel or complementary diamond model for CM. As such, it is similar to Figure C-1. To my knowledge, it is the first such model of its type for CM. Its purpose is to show the full range of interrelated activities for CM.

Figure C-2 shows that in a similar fashion to Figure C-1, the—or more accurately, *a*—diamond model for CM begins with the felt sense or recognition of a potential threat that is internal or external to an organization. At this point, the full nature of the threat is not known, just the sense that something

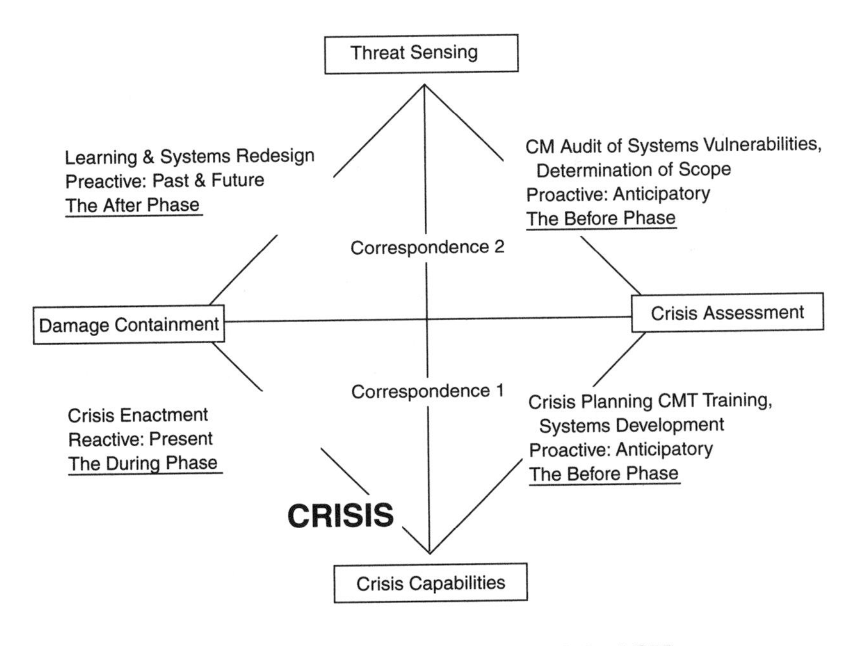

Figure C-2. The diamond model of CM: *Interactive* systems thinking.

is potentially remiss. The process of building a conceptual, or initial, model of the threat consists of using the model presented in Figure C-1 or something similar to it. That is, the model serves as a basis for conducting a crisis audit or a threat assessment of an organization.

The point is not that the model in Figure C-1 is the model for accomplishing this. The point is that something has to be used to perform an initial or a preliminary crisis audit in order for an organization to begin a systematic assessment of the threats and risks it is facing. The initial assessment sets the tone for all future efforts. It needs to be revised as one learns more, but it constitutes a crucial part of the "before" phase of CM.

The next phase consists of using the initial assessment to begin developing the necessary organizational capabilities to manage an actual crisis. In crisis plans, this generally means a trained CM team (CMT). It also includes crisis simulations.

Even with the best of plans, preparations, and capabilities, virtually all crisis experts and scholars agree that a major crisis is virtually guaranteed to happen to every organization. Thus, the following phase consists of enactment of an organization's crisis plans, preparations, and capabilities. This is the "during," or reactive, phase of CM. Damage containment is, in effect, parallel to the solution phase of scientific problem solving.

Finally, continual learning is the real test of an organization's ability and willingness to implement CM.

Notice that, as with the case of scientific problem solving, the definition of what is a crisis changes, often dramatically, as we move around the diamond model. In other words, the definition of what is and what is not a crisis cannot be decoupled from a systems model of crises. In the language of systems, the definition of critical terms and events is not separable from the process of diagnosing and treating them.

Note

1. The type I and type II errors can easily be explained as follows. Suppose that you are a drug company and that you have a new version of an older drug. You want to know if the new version is better than the old one. You test and compare both drugs on large samples of people. Since the samples can yield false results, you can make two kinds of errors. You can say that the new drug is better than the old one when it is not (the type II error), or that the old one is better than the new one when it is not (the type I error).

Index

About the Author

Dr. Ian Mitroff is the Harold Quinton Distinguished Professor of Business Policy at the Marshall School of Business, University of Southern California, and Professor of Journalism at The Annenberg School of Communications at USC. He was the founder of the USC Center for Crisis Management, which he directed for ten years. He is widely recognized as a founder of the discipline of crisis management.

As a teacher, writer, and consultant, Dr. Mitroff specializes in crisis prevention, strategic planning, and the design of ethical work environments.

He is the author of more than 300 articles and 26 books on a wide range of topics, including crisis management, corporate culture, business policy, current events, organizational change, and spirituality in the workplace. His most recent books include *A Spiritual Audit of Corporate America* and *Managing Crises Before They Happen*.

Dr. Mitroff is a frequent keynote speaker at national conventions of professional and public organizations and has lectured to corporate, academic, and government leaders in more than twenty countries. He has appeared on many national radio and television shows, including *Window on Wall Street*, CNN, and National Public Radio's *Marketplace*. He was a charter member of the Academy of Management's Journals Hall of Fame and has been a Fellow of the Academy of Management, the American Psychological Association, and the American Association for the Advancement of Science. In 1992–1993 he was president of the International Society for the Systems Sciences.

Ian Mitroff earned his B.A., M.S., and Ph.D. at the University of California, Berkeley. He also holds an honorary doctorate in philosophy from the University of Stockholm, Sweden.

AMA SEMINARS
people
to work
with you
AMA